THIRTEEN WAYS OF CROSSING THE PIAZZA:

COLLECTED POEMS

GUERNICA WORLD EDITIONS 19

THIRTEEN WAYS OF CROSSING THE PIAZZA: COLLECTED POEMS

Pellegrino D'Acierno

GUERNICA
World
EDITIONS

TORONTO—CHICAGO—BUFFALO—LANCASTER (U.K.)
2019

Michael Mirolla, editor
Cover design: Allen Jomoc Jr.
Interior layout: Jill Ronsley, suneditwrite.com
Cover image: *The Piazza as Mandala,* Lucio Pozzi
Interior illustrations: Lucio Pozzi
Guernica Editions Inc.
287 Templemead Drive, Hamilton (ON), Canada L6M 2Z7
2250 Military Road, Tonawanda, N.Y. 14150-6000 U.S.A.
www.guernicaeditions.com

Distributors:
Independent Publishers Group (IPG)
600 North Pulaski Road, Chicago IL 60624
University of Toronto Press Distribution,
5201 Dufferin Street, Toronto (ON), Canada M3H 5T8
Gazelle Book Services, White Cross Mills
High Town, Lancaster LA1 4XS U.K.

First edition.
Printed in Canada.

Legal Deposit—Third Quarter
Library of Congress Catalog Card Number: 2019944914
Library and Archives Canada Cataloguing in Publication
Title: Thirteen ways of crossing the piazza : collected poems / Pellegrino D'Acierno.
Other titles: Poems. Selections
Names: D'Acierno, Pellegrino, 1943- author.
Description: Series statement: Guernica world editions ; 19
Identifiers: Canadiana 20190110813 | ISBN 9781771834346 (softcover)
Classification: LCC PS3554.A237 A6 2019 | DDC 811/.6—dc23

Contents

Dedicated

To the incomparable Lucio Pozzi,
Supreme artist in both abstraction and realism
and dear friend and muse;

To Frank Lentricchia and Dante Matelli,
Grandi maestri della scrittura
e amici per la pelle;

And, once again, to the necessary angels—
Sam Pellegrino and Giada

THIRTEEN WAYS OF CROSSING THE PIAZZA

R

A **O**

M

I

... through backwards
vehemently as music
to reverse
the karma-bearing wheel
another wrack
like sunlight or madness
past the abiding coitus of
word and world
to where silence takes place
more vehemently than music

The roisterous Romans
stain the silence
with their first Amen
—Ma vammoriammazzato!—
that punctuates the siesta
and begins their nightsong

Their damned blessing
at once consecrates and breaks
the moment of epoché
that suspends
the happening of the world

As the evening deepens
will the delirious and endless drifting
though the labyrinth
of the piazza
lead to the trap
of Via di Testa Spaccata
—the sinister street of no return
that no longer exists—
or will the *divagamento*

grant the joy of profane illuminations
or even open to enlightenment?

The rambunctious nocturne
of Carnevale
kills the silence once and for all
as the violently pullulating piazza
becomes the people's theater
and midnight installs the proletarian night

In the philosopher's tale
according to the skeptical Lucretius
nothing can be made of nothing . . .
but according to nature
exquisite flowers can be made
of excrement
and according to G.G. Belli
—poet of the belly of Rome
Pope and Pimp of the piazza
voice of the voiceless and the negated—
exquisite sonnets can be made
from the rough language of the skin,
ABBA ABBA from the cacophony
of the vulgar and obscene dialect
of the Roman streets
blessing us with their deafening last Amens
and liberating the body-and-soul's ear
by deranging the monotony of line
and violating the tyranny of rhyme
(despite the necessary Amen—
CDE/CDE)

Embedded within the aftershocks
of the street prophet's blasts
—Chi vva la notte, va a la morte—
is the secret of ROMA/AMOR:
the chaotic play of the piazza
breaks the mandala into fragments

and turns the soul of the world
topsy-turvy and inside-out,
the ritornello becomes a vicious circle
and everything must be done
backwards and against the grain
the Bacchanalia is performed
in the name of Christ—

wine
confetti
lightness
pietas
eros
carpe noctem
odi et amo
Evoe!

displace

blood
nails
gravity
caritas
agape
carpe diem
amo et odi
Hallelujah!

the flagrancy of bones and flesh

The sacred masquerades as the profane
the profane as the sacred
and the dangerous excess
of the orgy becomes the work of God

After the second midnight has passed
when will Carnevale end?
Ciao Bacchus! Ciao Ggesummaria!
Ciao Culiseo! Ciao epoché!

Now the perfect torque
of mardi gras spends itself
in the last fling of confetti
and the revelers' dying laughter
—acetylene through the teeth of masks—
grants congé to all
then in nuances of rose
the dayspring severs
remorselessly
the night-face of Eurydice perhaps

To cross the piazza
my liminal steps
trample the dead ends of things
and to mime the Orphic howl
I fling outwards the flagrancy
of bones and flesh

The new body
wordless
reckless
hand in hand
with the amorous open
and its intricate rigadoon
of earth and sky, of gods and mortals

The charm is wound up in traces circlewise

Once again
remorselessly
the fierce world
configures itself
as the bounding line
of dung and azure

Within Sant'Agnese in Agone
the needle-eyed supplicants
kowtow to receive
the perfect face of death
and the fabulous fever of ashes—
asterisks of the *semper eadem*,
those orthodox paradises always-already lost

[*Martedì Grasso*/Ash Wednesday]

Piranesi and the great theatre of the world

II

In Rome nothing is primal
it is already dawn
Venus Pronuba is furious
at being caught in the nakedness
of the evening star
it is already no longer dawn
Profane Venus is furious
at being caught
in the chaste zone
of the morning star,
primed for her rendezvous
with the idiot day

In the beginning was the last word
—*otium* (leisure)—
inextricably linked to the first word
—*negotium* (work)—

Within the dizzying violet noise
—collisions of octaves—
of the piazza
how is one to find
the way to silence
that leads to *otium philosophandi*
and the dismantling of wisdom?
in the false movement
of the pulsating piazza
where is one to execute
the dangerous swerve
that leads irrevocably
from idleness to worthy leisure,
what Cicero called "*otium cum dignitate*"
and what the ever-more-decadent Romans
now call oblivion?

In Rome it is always-already
the Sabbath of the great cosmic tedium
even the deus ex machina is idling
in the archaic torso of the river god
—bearded lethargic Baroque
and depleted of all scenarios of the new—
Priced for immediate sale
on a makeshift easel
the second state of Piranesi's *Carceri IX*
creaks and groans
as it raises once again the apparatus
of the great theatre of the world

the marionettes and Rome drawn and quartered

In the beginning was the fratricide
the she-wolves and vestals
the cut-throats and gods sleep it off
in the system of solitudes
it is time for the fall out of time

As always the already-desired
capital ALL
—mundum and Darstellung—
is drawn and quartered
by the marionettes who work
the pater-noster machine
the infinite body of Pan
is torn asunder and scattered
in the earth-working path

In the beginning was the orgy
and in its violent farce Pulcinella will play Christ

In the beginning and in the ending
is the exorbitance of the masquerade
Now Rome is Rome
Now Rome becomes a destiny

Rome's splendor to be eternally sung
in an elegy by Propertius
—"Stranger, look your fill!"—
the madness of her wisdom
to be danced to an ecstatic drum
in honor of Minerva
—she who measures—
Rome's sacred violence to be endured
by the raped Sabine women and
the decapitated Saint Agnes
and, in Rome after Rome,
by their celluloid sisters
Pina and Mamma Roma

Rome's mystery to be rendered
Socratic at the feast of the
reclining gods whose
drunkenness renders the
piazza into an aporia
—a circle of which
the center is everywhere
and the circumference is nowhere—
Rome's eternal fallenness
to be again confirmed
by the street-saint Accattone
—pimp and parasite—
who staggers
through the City of God
to establish being-towards-death

To cross the piazza
—even when hearing
a voice at one's back—
one cuts a beginning
here and now
in any-place-whatsoever
indifferently
and with the blind magnitudes
of body and soul
for there and then one comes back again

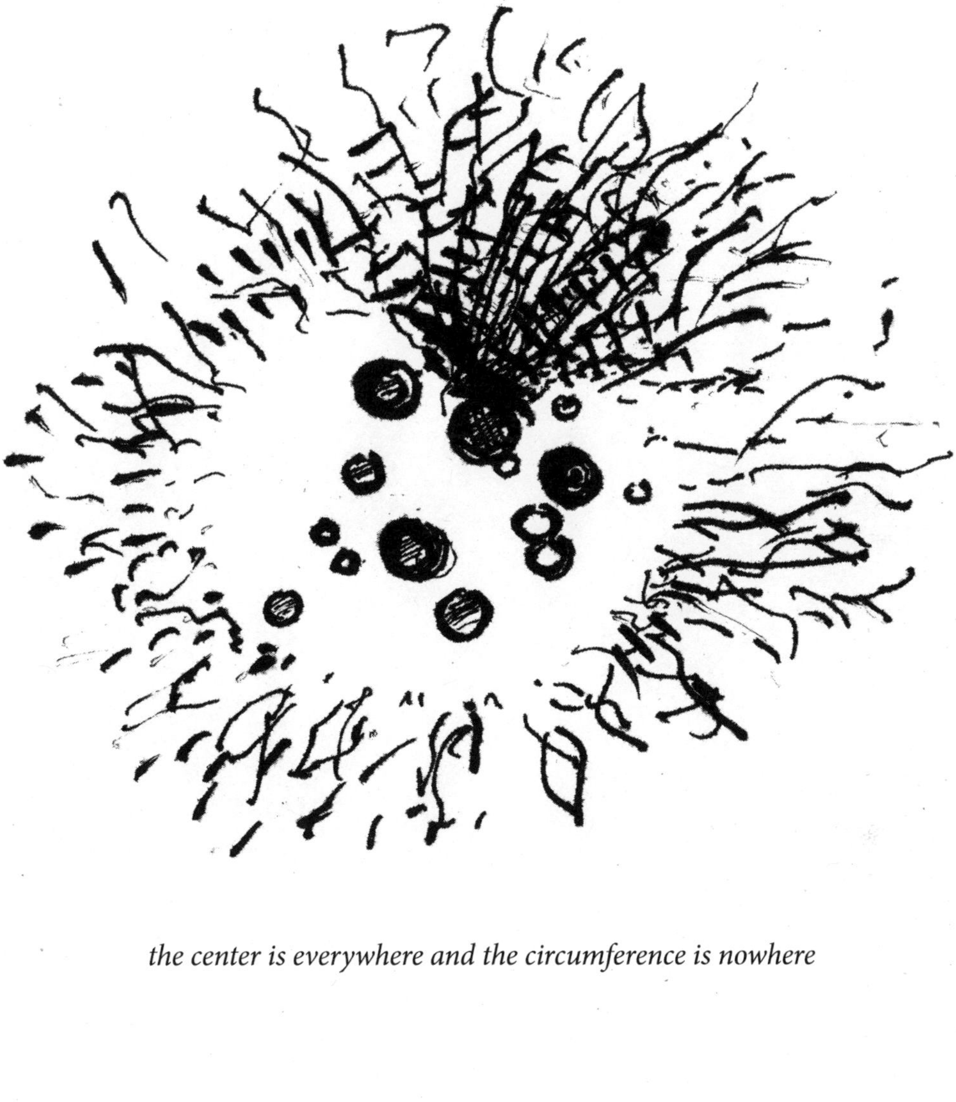

the center is everywhere and the circumference is nowhere

In default of a gambit
and ignorant of Venus's
slowly mounting delirium
the squid-seller
with a raucous shout
slits once again
the oculus of the sun

[Lauds]

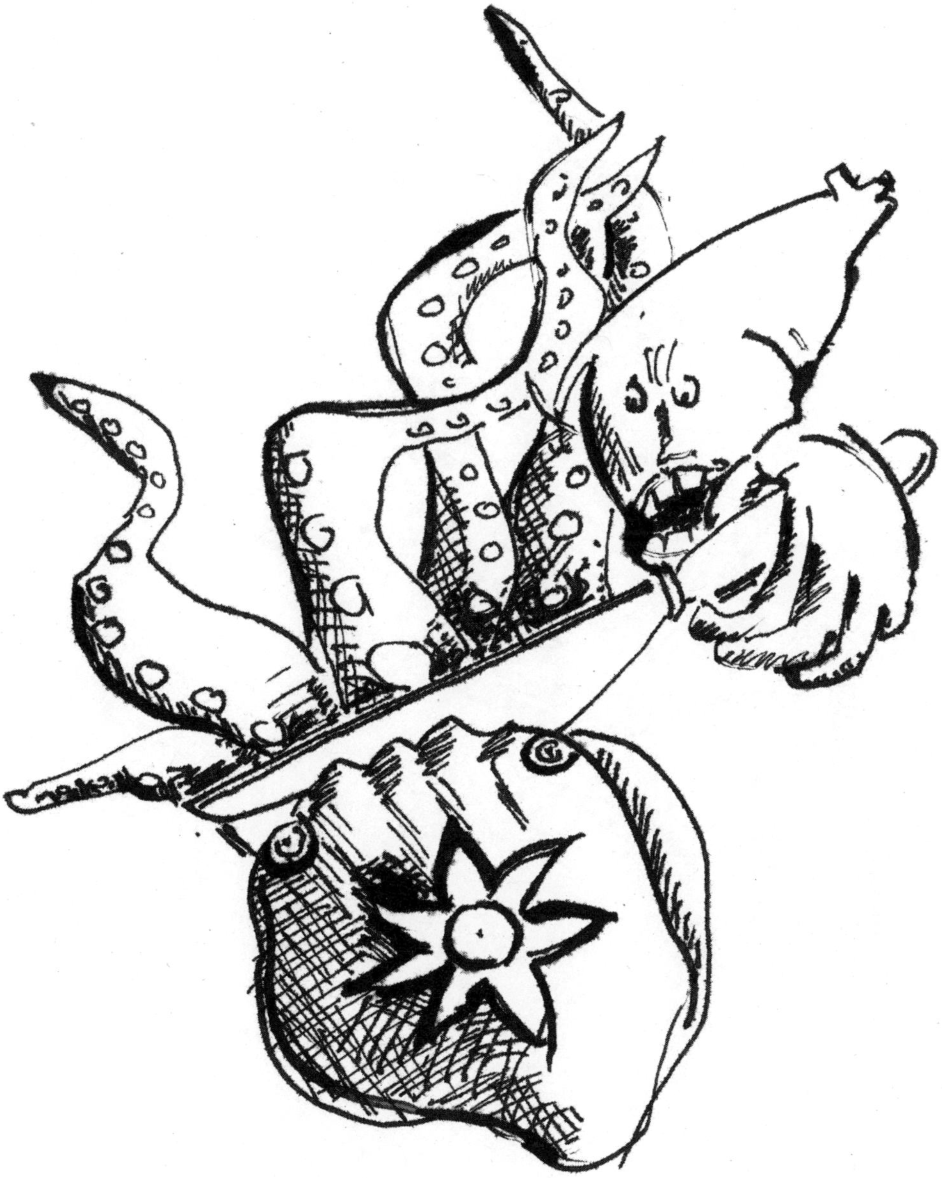

the squid-seller slits once again the oculus of the sun

Saint Agnes decapitated and her celluloid sisters
(the genealogy of sacred violence toward the women of Rome
that leads to the aristocratic self-martyrdom of La Contessa Violante P.)

III

The Contessa Violante P.
black aristocrat and soothsayer of the place
commands the Piazza Navona
with her imperious Roman nose
as if it were her salon
and dismisses with the scarab
of her index finger
the entire twentieth-century
on the misoneistic grounds
that it is disfigured in its proportions
and by its general lack of style,
having broken the state by abolishing
the pre-Jacobin rule of noblesse-oblige

With the leniencies of her black Capri shawl
she plays hide-and-seek
with her remnant beauty
—genre diaphane—
the copine being one of her many personae,
the one in which she slept with the enemy
without, as she is quick to point out, betraying
the immaculate politics
of her class—Ghibellinissima—

Every morning chez Tre Scalini
(the rearmost table for she is partial
to what she has baptized the Garbo strip)
after exorcising the chartreuse
body of night
with a blood orange
and three thimbles of espresso
—ristrettissimo—
she hisses forth

in *erre moscia*
her legend for all to hear,
the aria of Hecate who rules
over the crossroads of the piazza:

—To saunter is a minor art of the city,
  a mere extension of the philosophy of clothes
  for which you English chastise us Romans
  but to which you are not immune.
  I assume you are English,
  perhaps a swain of Zuleika Dobson,
  but definitely not a barbarous Yankee.

the explosion of carnal surfaces and the faulty clock

Your nostrils give you away,
the irony with which you inflect
your inter-sententials.
But there is a world of difference between
our art of masquerade and your pufferie
which, when all is said and done, is but
ascetic play, an expression of recusancy
and your famous puritanism,
an ethical revolt in fieri.
We Romans, instead, are the people
of the gorgeous spectacle
and the decorum of *la bella figura … fi-gu-ra.*
Kant said we Italians are incapable
of experiencing the sublime.
But our exaggerated cult of beauty
—the opulent elegance immanent
in the explosion of carnal surfaces—
is far more dangerous than
the terror imminent in the sublime.

Please excuse these impertinent stereotypes,
do I offend? They are the *sciochezze*
one prattles in the morning … ipse dixit
I drink Pernod only when the Scirocco blows.
It appeases the noia,
the malicious devil
in the faulty clock
that affixes the night body to the day body.
The fall of Rome is eternal.
Our history is made of Chinese boxes:
what appeared to have been the Age of Mussolini,
in turn, appeared to have been the Age of Croce
and, in turn, to have been the Age of Gramsci …
and so on. *Capisce, Lei?*
Così, I became a Communist
not to be thrown out of my palazzo …
in caude venom and carve your mask, comrade—

As he deposits a tartufo at the table
of the man sporting a Turnbull & Asser cravat
the waiter, an out of work tenor,
intones:

"*Come la Tosca in teatro* ..."

[Prime]

IV

High Noon:
the truculent tabbies,
mesmerizing gangsters of perception,
lap the intricate herring-bones
of diminishing shadow

Backfire explodes
like an oracle
from the idling of a red Ferrari
trapped within the visored phalanx
of gridlocked Fiats on the Corso
to incite lost time's
insidious harangue:

The gala days of one Caesar too many
sullen Caligula pomping the dazzle of Venus
the ludic teeth of the ancient horde
the spectacle of thumbs
the black-shirted salutes of the slaughterers
the herd's jargon lashing the dead
into their orbit:
HABET! HOC HABET!

The midnight of day: sun-blindness
the severe parenthesis
of the piazza
(cogito)
and paradises
elemented
in the cloacal stench of ruins
and further down the course
of skin-deep roads leading to Rome,
the panic of entrails and tongues

stung
by the commanding thunder
of Jove
into the more human ratio
of cosmic piety and dead silence,
Roma, caput mundi, caput mortuum

[Sext]

teeth of ancient hordes, thumbs and salutes, entrails and tongues

V

With Goethe's *Italienische Reise*
for a Baedeker
and dressed in the stark perfections
of black
the flâneur
connoisseur of surfaces
lolls his afternoon mastery over place
and pivots his omnipotence
before the virtual mirror
of the piazza,
the supreme place to see and be seen

Impresario of the city of eyes
he stalks the Vedic crowd
thrashing its antic flesh
with the adagios of his gothic gaze

From nowhere a lode-face unfurls
its demonic glass
Beatrice, Bice, Bi
the rogue angel of the drift
the madonna of loopholes and vignettes
widowing and maidening
beckons to the brave man:
—Sia ammazato chi non fa l'amore!—

Prince Vogelfrei
a Rembrandt exposed to the sun
is impaled by her glance
his dandiacal body
stiffens into a cruel tap dance
and veers across the piazza
to assume a visage

ad libitum

Within the violent event of the South wind,
the bridle of Narcissus,
the teeth of the Scirocco
nibble at the face of man

(piazzando in the asylum of the open-air café
Jimmie Hands, a.k.a. Jimmie Thorns,
the Nietzsche of Bleecker Street,
skyscraper soul with a Prix de Rome,
notes in the adverseria of his espresso cup:
"The dandy, understood as the paradigm
of exigent writing, was one of his
several scriptural personae ...")

[None]

the black flies

VI

After the insomnia of day
when the children's handhold dance
at last renders
alphabetic and fabulous
the intractable stillness
that the siesta has hung in its wake

When the vibrato of Santaccia's
preliminary street-aria
of reckless blood
penetrates deeper than grappa
into the thick digits
of the old men playing at morra

When the superstitious Salii
stop their leaping
to prepare a charm
against thunder and lightning
performed with onions
and hair and pilchards

When the black flies
buzz the knots of excrement,
the spoors of the bolting sun

Then the deep logos
the flesh-made-word
must be lingering
in the susurrus void
of the piazza:

To crossover
Jack be nimble
Jack be quick
Jack be onomatopoeic:
rhyme to the nick of time
what is made of dust and lust
of tunc and nunc
the Roman candle of Mutunus Tutunus

[Vespers]

VII

Incipit: the commotion of the passeggiata
resounds within the funnel
of the Piazza Navona

In the Rome of incalculable inertia
all days under the sign of canicola
are intercalary
only the premonitions
of the ponentino
and the jags of espresso
animate the swarm
infusing Zeit with Geist

What lures us more
into the prison house of ennui
the boondoggling
of the lava-black cobblestones
—abacus of peppercorns—
or the yellow voice
of the peddler of almanacs
and their opium of years?

Lacrimae rerum:
tears lacerating
the lineaments of all things;
here the spleen of history writes itself
in the bleeding ochre-wash of walls

The Rome of the Caesars
and the Rome of the Popes
have become a bazaar:
the gold-toothed hawkers
rip the winds from Eden

with the plastic howl
of their five-and-dime bullroarers,
chartreuse and magenta merchandise,
and whip the sinews
of the crowd
into the bitch carioca of time
Now the provincial town
masquerades as the metropolis
—site of supreme alienation—
obliging its citizens
to ignore its shocks
by assuming soigné
and cosmopolitan postures
and the blasé masks requisite
for drifting through
the mesmerizing spectacles
of la dolce vita

and yet it is written in stone:
Rome is not simply a great city,
it is the city and the world

Urbi et Orbi

(and inscribed elsewhere—
stupenda e misera città"—
and elsewhere in displaced form—
"*non donna di provincia, ma bordello*")

Nonetheless,
movement remains a Heraclitan farce,
another travesty of the place
even the Second Paradox
is part of the burlesque
the players from Trastevere
assume their Punch and Judy positions
and with a drum roll
the Lazzo of Zeno commences:
Meo-Patacca, that human bludgeon,

hen-steps swift as Achilles
to swoop down
on the shuffling Marco-Pepe
who makes an oblique bee-line
for the obelisk
dog-mathematicians both,
they slip on zeroes
then belly-flop
and sprawl like turtles on their backs
while the children cudgel them with guffaws
and put coins in their mouths

Roma, capital of noia,
—the anger incarcerated in boredom,
and vented through dolce far niente—
sun-heap of dead ends
and false beginnings,
labyrinth of multitude and solitude,
where the fear that prompts the mad journey
is lulled to sleep
in the Caffè Omphalos

the mathematical dog

Four Rivers, the lion and the horse

Even the insatiable desire
of the many-bodied Ulysses dozes,
fascinated by the
blissful song cascading
from the fountain of the river gods
the river that is four rivers
from time to time
and always
folds into infinity

It is only the white horse
and lion of wrath
that bite with travertine and foam
into his infinite dream
to confound
the bodies of Calypso, Circe, and Penelope
thereby keeping his mad desire alive
and headed toward a destiny

The hurricane of pigeons,
lumpen-fowls,
lacerates the piazza with guano …

[Compline]

VIII

My guide, the illustrious and gentilissimo
Professore Palindrome,
the most enlightened man
of the far left in Rome
but nonetheless terribly elegant
as correct in his dress as in his syntax,
takes me by the arm
—the masculine protocol of the piazza—
informing me,
in an aside that approaches gossip,
of the dapper man who approaches us
arm-in-arm with his retinue:
Peripatētici

Man of the faux pas,
the old aesthete resides in several floors
of an old palazzo on the Via Giulia
an insatiable collector,
a Roman Citizen Kane, you know,
the nine Venuses and twenty-six Virgins
the walls are always collapsing
from the weight of things
now he has decorated an entire
wall of the piano nobile
with a vast collection of fedoras and trilbys
although in general a man well-liked in Rome,
—simpatico in the eyes
of *apocaliptici* and *integrati* alike—
he is taken for a *iettatóre*
by the plebes
who refuse to mention his name—

Averting his gaze, my guide
salutes him as one of his tribe
and thus with tongue in cheek
—*Bacio le mani, Maestro,*
  regards to the Borsalino—
and, after passing, immediately instructs me
to touch metal and then my privates,
another protocol of the place
If it were permitted, I would speak to him;
since it is not, my gaze asks:
—Carissimo,
with what truffles and raspberries
of discourse
do you fascinate the two vestals
whose limbs Venus-strain
to rein in the rebellious leashes
of the snow-white borzoi?
with what sottovoce
or ghost dance of words
do you command and refine
your sweet, lynx-eyed company?

What pillow-book or
law of a Tobias-night
do you gloss
to lead the new brides
to blush like the sunset?
do you hold out to them
the perfect mirror of Narcissus
the glass into which Sussana
turned out the manna
of her ideal nakedness
to the idiotic and boorish elders
who, shuddering in the spindle
of their groins,
sever the body of the dreamer
from the dream?—

The contra-tempo:
behind his back
a Romanaccio kisses him with
flicks of the ear
this impertinence
—penisissimo—
no longer recognizes
the routines of the cicisbeo,
the virtuoso of one string
the magnifico of the infinite conversation.
Rome has never learned
Diotima's subtle art of ladders,
preferring instead Cagliostro
and the mandrake climatic between sheets

To cross the piazza
the Maestro executes a cunning minuet
and without progressing a single step
ends up easily on the very spot
whence he began

From the balcony
the slit-tongue of the nightingale
caged in a boudoir of bougainvillea
gives the *pernacchia* to silence,
to all the most exquisite solecism of all

[Nocturne: The Book of Hours Sleeps]

IX

Incipit: Trimalchio's Feast

Ferragosto (Augustus' rest),
harvest is announced
by the summer fare alla romana
—fiori di zucca fritti
and *pasta alla checca—*
to be devoured al fresco
as part of the dance with the sky

Semper Saturnalia agunt

In the beginning was the feast
—not to have but to be—
the complete stranger that I am is welcomed
by the host to a feast in progress
at the trattoria without a name—
hence its nickname, the "Famous Trattoria"

Here the solarity of the South reigns:
not to eat and carouse in excess
would be an insult
and finally I am a proper Roman

Here the scenario of Roma/Amor
is most fully enacted:
here everyone is immediately
given the "tu"
and thus a face

The satura/the satire

Our Trimalchio
assigns us names:

Catullus, Petronius, and Propertius
(accompanied by his beloved Cynthia
who remains unnamed)
Belli, Trilussa, and Moravia
(together with both his "wives"
Dacia and Elsa
upon whose hands
the bowing Trimalchio bestows air kisses)
and Gadda, nicknamed that "Aweful Mess"

Pier Paolo Pasolini and Mamma Roma
Marcello accompanied by the Sylvia
of the kiss interruptus
in the Fontana di Trevi
Marcello again,
this time by himself and blue,
abandoned by Mara of Rome
and stalked by the flagrant memory
of her striptease
executed in an apartment
with a bird's eye view of the piazza
the Great Fellini
with Giulietta and Claudia
fastened to his hat
and to each of his arms
the Great Antonioni and Monica,
the Madonna of the Eclipse
as effected through montage
And the two momentary exiles:
Gore Vidal and Clint Eastwood

No Caesar or Pope is appointed
to reign in the anarchy

At the separate table
for the pimps
who remain unnamed
and for the antipatici
whom he does name
he places Encolpius and Ascyltos
with little Giton sitting between them
so the trio can express
their aristocratic disdain
for the vulgar spectacle
and show off their *"al dentismo"*
by ridiculing the chef's fatal gaffe
of overdone and flaccid
penne alla carbonara
and the unpardonable
absence of *puntarelle*
the blades are only impressed
by the palate cleanser—
a fig ingeniously topped
by a thin layer of crystalized ice
infused with grappa

Non semper Saturnalia erunt

Here even that greatest of parasites,
la commare secca,
the Madonna of Death,
is made drunk
and rendered unable to cross the piazza
Here even the virtuous Epicurus
forsakes his search for ataraxia

Holding a glass of Falernium
in his right hand,
the hunchbacked guest
nicknamed Antonio Gramsci
—actually an angry *ragazzo di vita*—
performs a wicked street rant

in the tumultuous form of a "blitzkrieg bop"
accompanied by a Tympana
and punctuated by the shrill sounds
of a Tintinnabulum

—Ciak!
Chew on this forever:
Every man and every woman
is a philosopher.
Drink this down fast:
We are a country of geniuses—
geniuses like Vittorio Emanuele III,
the Savoia king who ran away
on September 8th, 1943;
the Italian generals who changed allies
at the last minute
(May 23, 1915 and September 3, 1943).
We never finished a war with
the ally we started with.

But that's Italy and its broken genius:
our history takes place
as panem et circenses
as ludi and slapstick in the Circus Maximus
expanded into the world.
Romulus killed Remus
Brutus and Cassius
and their accomplices
assassinated Caesar
with the slashes
of twenty-three Roman daggers
Cola di Rienzo was pierced
by the thousand daggers
of the deranged crowd.
Zounds! Zlids! Znails! ad nauseam
as the slow apocalypse unfolds

Later on in the ricorso
Giacomo Matteoti, the White Knight
who denounced the Black-shirted violence
of the miles gloriosus,
was kidnapped and
stabbed to death
with a blunt carpenter's file
and in the black comedy
scripted by the heirs of Plautus
the supreme alazons
—the Nazis—
inured by cognac
shot in the back of the head
three hundred and thirty-five Roman partisans
in the Ardeatine massacre

history may repeat itself
—first as trompe-l'œil, then as black painting;
  first as a charm
  against thunder and lightning,
  then as the "Steel-Pact"—

but it always remains Janus-faced
looking backward to Caesarism
and forward to Hamletism

Ciak!
Goddess, stand with me
as I chant this vulgar jeremiad
to voice my refusal
to be an accomplice
to the silence
imposed by the instrumentum regni
—Give us this day our daily prolefeed—

as you walk past the Ara Pacis
in your armored bodies
stunted by the failure to rebel
listen and you shall hear
sizzling through
the solemn Re Gesti of Augustus
written in cold stone
the howls of a danse macabre—

"*Oh mia Patria sì bella e perduta*!
O membranza sì cara e fatal!"

"*Ma la Gloria non vedo*."

"*La parola ITALIA deve*
dominare sulla parola LIBERTÀ"

"*Eia eia alalà*"

"*Strage e melancholia*"

Janus power over two-faced history and the Ardeatine massacre

Ciak!
We produced everything
from the Pope to the Mafia,
from Do Re Mi … to the roar of a red Ferrari
And now we specialize in the Republican
who rallies for the king, the pious atheist,
the democratic fascist, the virgin whore,
the capitalist commie, the Yankee haters
who send their children to Harvard,
and finally, the teachers who take their
scholarship students to Auschwitz and Dachau
(a tear is good for a photo-op)
and then go pay a visit to Mussolini's tomb
with the whole class

Ciak!
Hope to see you again before Doom's Day.
If not, you'll find me in hell:
a cousin of mine is a fire attendant there
and will treat us better
than some church-going son of a bitch
who is sitting on his ass in Paradise.
Remember to visit my ashes
in the Protestant Cemetery
and, on your way, do genuflect
to the dark statue of Giordano Bruno
that enlightens the Campo de' Fiori
by multiplying the sun
Ciak!—

Now multiplied, carnivalized,
and liberated
by the great communion
of Trimalchio's lectisternium
and its vast pun
—This is my body
that no longer requires a name—
I finally become an improper

and thus true Roman
    Populusque
a Romanaccio on a roll
—“*Li mortacci tua*!”—
and register with laughter
the wrath in Trimalchio’s last toast

—To my wife, Fortunata,
  who will not weep at my funeral:
  do not kiss me when I am dead!

  To my dear friends:
  “God, if only these stones would turn into bread!”—

After one-too-many rounds of *ammazzacaffè*
—the lethal Picolit Grappa—
(the umbrae exclaim:
“Down with the banal
Sambuca con la mosca!”)
the guests join in a Bacchanalian procession
to cross the piazza
on their way to celebrate
Trimalchio’s mock funeral.

Their midnight state obliges them to
avoid the challenge of ascending
the steep sacred stairs
leading to the Aracoelia
and, instead, they follow
the blonde traces
of Anita Ekberg
as she tangos up
the more welcoming and
secular cordonnata
to the Campidoglio

The celebrants remain totally oblivious
to the admonitory honking
of the sacred geese around Juno’s temple

Lying down on an unfolded newspaper
—his ephemeral tomb—
in front of the statue
of the noble Marcus Aurelius,
the meta-dead Trimalchio
begins to carve his mask
as the meta-mourners await
his meta-resurrection

[The Book of Hours Dies]

Trimalchio's Funeral

X

QUEM QUARITUS …

deranged
by the absolute
whiskey of midnight and
having lost the straight way to
Canterbury or Mecca or Delphi or Jerusalem
the piebald mass of pilgrims makes the stop-time
stations of the piazza: sleeping beauties from Parioli
pursue the vicarious chocolate of night straining at the
leashes of their chaperones, popes of peroxide and angels with
trompe l'oeil genitals assume their usual perches on the sinister
side of Bernini's fountain where they squander their amorous signs,
jazzmen, late of Harlem and now holed up chez Brick Top's
unleash the wicked blues of their tight exile
while, keeping time, * the sent Romans—ever chic and
poncif—imprison the * * decline of the West in their
miserere shimmy, * innocents abroad,
the decorous troop of Japanese bow
their kimono bodies in unison to
the falling star, one of their number
who has mistaken Frascati R for saki, goes moon fishing
like Basho * * in the fountain
of Neptune A O more innocents,
the pezzi arrichiti, sons * * of the Brooklyn Bridge, track
with their Cadillac shoes M the slender sandal-prints
of their imaginary ancestors, somewhat cautiously
for they like the apprehensive river
gods await the collapse of Borromini's
conceited facade * as foretold by their
cicerone who digs— * * American Express—
her Beltrami spikes * into the rough cob-
blestones like a drum majorette/
goaded by the octopus moon
the great round-dance of the stranger-gods
begins: gold hunters, amen hunters, frisson hunters,
futurism-of the-Pope hunters, totem hunters,
arcanum-of-the-commodity hunters, omen
hunters, indulgence hunters, two-of-
a-kind hunters and still sharper
e hunters after all these hunters: a noi
noi all are welcome for in Rome is the
antri the gods are wont to dance of the
we are assume the guise morti di fame,
treated of strangers tarantella
and do of cuthroats
treat as and she/
wolves

… O CRISTICOLAE?

[The Book of Hours Carouses]

XI

First Duet: Singing the Counter-Hegemonic Blues

Who comes to Rome and never sees the Pantheon returns an ass.

The two former golden boys
surge onto the piazza
as if they were revolutionaries,
occupying it as they did College Walk
when they were graduate students
at Kojumbia University in '68

They are now looking for a revolution
in a nation that has only produced
revolutions manqués
in the late afternoon they attend
with the workers and university students
a lecture on the time of monsters

Determined to be more
than cultural adventurers
in pursuit
of the rigorous magic
of the piazza
or archi-tourists
attempting to rid themselves
of piazza-envy
they scribble with black chalk
a graffitto on an ochre wall—
Non sono un artista, sono un operaio

The long-haired self-exiles
—one a screenwriter manqué,
the other a poet manqué;

both revolutionaries without a revolution—
slow down to execute
a randonnée
in which they search to overhear
radical sprach
—Romans, countrymen, and lovers—
hoping to connect with their comrades,
the band of young and angry red bodies
that performs
through a secretive and silent rally
the politics of the piazza
in the Years of Lead
Where have you gone Julius Caesar?
Et tu, Brute? Then fall, Pier Paolo Pasolini

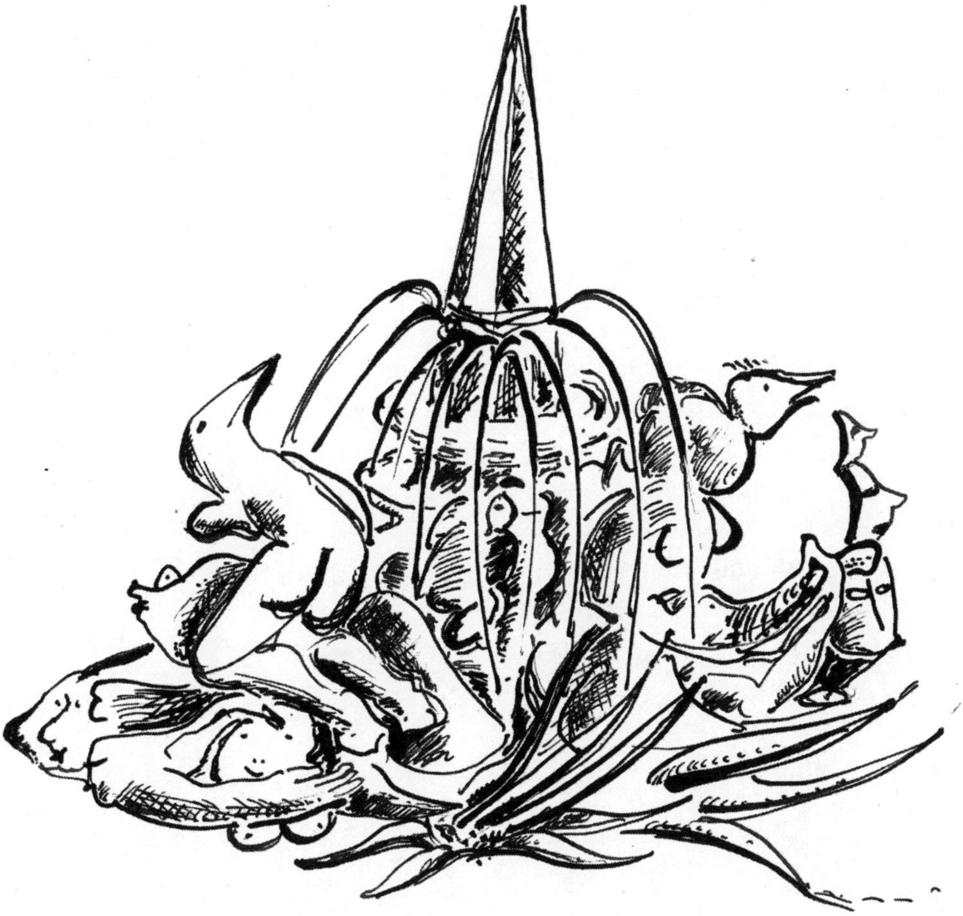

bodies on fire under the Fountain

Instead of blasts of incendiary talk,
they are accosted by a barrage of piropos
—benignly flirtatious without being scatological—
aimed at the daughters of Venus,
tiptoeing across the piazza
in golden Gucci sandals,
by the gang of polymorphously perverse
sons of Mars
who are immediately disarmed
by the bitter honey
of their goddesses' indifference

The two mavericks' search for the political other,
that is, the political other within themselves,
has been derailed by the satyrs manqués
and then is terminated by the unruly crowd
that realizes the revolution
—spontaneously and unknowingly—

Prompted by a group of street musicians
named Liber Pater
the people perform
their art of protest
by chanting
in unison "Bella ciao"
and by dancing
as a multitude
to its furious rhythms
that kill the spirit of gravity
even though they lead
the brave partisan from love to death

Everyone joins in the carnival,
their bodies set on fire
by the retro-anthem
as it resonates
across the three fountains,
turning diamat

into one more masquerade

All differences are momentarily eliminated
by the intermingling of men and women
of all ages and all social classes—
patricians, plebeians,
gròssi, borghesi,
lazzaroni and morti di fame,
citizens and extracomunitarians,
pagans and Christians—
Cato the Censor is rendered speechless
as the ecstatic dance of the multitude

the vortex on fire—Who will carry the vision forward?

creates a manifesto in the form of noise,
an insurrection in the form of a collision

The moment of revelry
—the radical miracle in the piazza—
tells them clearly the truism:
make theater, not revolution
mayhem, not amen and amen

The crowd scatters
the war of maneuver
turns into a strange loop
and the moment is lost
in the vortex of the piazza
Who will carry the vision forward?

The pairs of lovers move
to the side streets
to catch their breath
leading the two rogues
to the Pasquino
where they are prompted
to scribble graffiti
on a previously posted pasquinade:

"Poets of the world unite!"
"Pier Paolo Pasolini must not die!"

Returning to the silent piazza
and the melancholy
of the concluded circus
they fancy themselves
charlatans of lust
and hipsters of desire
and give themselves up
to the frissons of flânerie

they want to be orphans
but remain avatars
of Odysseus and Aeneas:
one—the Tuscan—in search of a nostos;
the other—the New Yorker—in search
of the promised land,
even though they know Nietzsche by heart

They drift across the piazza and
with panache
assume their contemporary personae
—Robert Mitchum and Marlon Brando—
their dashing lookalikes

They search for Roman fever
amidst the confetti of the crowd's laughter—
where have the frenetic masqueraders
and agents provocateurs gone?
"Sia ammazzato chi non porta un moccolo!"
Who will carry the vision forward?

They cross the piazza haltingly
with their lowered gazes
fixed before their feet
even though the full moon
lifts up the chandeliers
to fashion a starry night

They stop to watch a group of old Romans
gathered around a bench
playing vociferously at knucklebones
their fascination is rewarded
by the courteous invitation
from the gamblers
to throw the dice—
the unlucky Mitchum casts a Vulture Throw
the lucky Brando a Venus Throw—
who will be the master of revels tonight?

After confronting the incalculable
they make an about face and
reminisce about their passeist professors
chastising them
not for their pedantic logic-chopping
and nose-picking (sic)
but for their failure to practice
a pedagogy of love

And then they pull to a halt:

"Procul, O procul este profani!"

The swaggering Mitchum, "n.a.r.",
intones bluntly but with sprezzatura

—Why speak of
those anti-metaphysical bastards,
those docents of micro-fascism,
when the piazza offers us
the promise of freedom
and mastery over the soul-fire?
Why let them triumph by permitting them
to ramble with us as we cross the piazza?

Tomorrow we shall go to Lake Nemi
to find the Golden Bough
and, afterwards, to sample
the volcanic wild strawberries—

**[Circa Mezzanotte:
The Book of Hours Interrupted
by the Hijacking of the Piazza]**

* * * * * * * *

Second Duet: Never Sing an Aria to Someone who Cannot Sing One to You in Return

Earlier in the day
the sky over the piazza
was rendered apocalyptic
by the dark shroud formed
by the furiously rotating
flocks of starlings

vertigo zoom … the effect
of the lacerated azure sky

The *bufera infernal* runs its course
it is the hour of duets

As the night empties out the piazza
the street musicians track the lingering lovers
with "Bye, Bye Blackbird"
and the fire-eater
spumes his last arc of flame

In the caffé,
the inside of the outside,
Francesca silently nurses her
slow Cuba Libre while Paolo,
Bogarting his last Lucky Strike,
does all the fast-talking

Then like fastidious pedants
they perform with their gazes
an exegesis of Canto Five of the *Inferno*
in the scholastic version of carpe noctem
she assumes the role of a Dantista
while he plays Henry Wadsworth Longfellow
defending the correctness of his translation:

"Kissed me upon the mouth all palpitating"

They perform together in silence
its correction:

"All trembling
he kissed my mouth
all trembling"

It is the foreplay
to a night of dangerous love
in which they enact
the profane implications of the
word "bocca"
and cross the piazza
blissfully

[Notturno: The Book of Hours Caresses]

the hunchbacked saint with the thousand starlings

XII

The white nights of the old poet
in extremis
culminate in the last rounds of the piazza
—his so-called nocturnal constitutional
together with aqua vitae—
hunchbacked with melancholy
he is given to frequent satyr leaps
as he closes down the piazza

He addresses
the epigoni and the stragglers
and ragazze di vita
in a thunderous voice
that precipitates landslides:

—Silence!
Call me Jonah and I will be your poet.
I'll fit you with a retro-Pasquinade
for twenty black years of art and song
in the great black belly of the white whale.
From outside, the light called for the harpoon
when all I had were lapsus calamai
and the will-to-métier
to purify the language of the tribe
when the tribe was committing obscene crimes.
Così, my obituary will read
that he renovated poetry
by articulating the poem of silence
within the poem of the words
and celebrated the gaiety
of the body
like a good Dionysian;
that he failed to distance himself from

the regime;
that he failed to cut the strings
of the puppeteer, old Lantern-Jaw;
that he was one of those who remained
chained to his divan chez Plato's cave
and who sipped prosecco
polemically but silently
at the bar of the Grand Hotel Abyss—

So be it …
No mention will be made
of my bludgeoning
of both the vulgare illustre
and the jargon of the piazza
No mention of the castor oil
I administered to the solipsistic
and flatulent rhetoric
through which the Caesars hoodwinked
the people once again

Save your praise for dead poets and dead poetry
If Fascism was a fist in the face,
I returned the blow
with the white space
between the words and
subtle catechresis,
whispers and deviations
that strike the soul

The freedom of poetry involves
another form of violence—
the soft violence of metaphor

[Vigiliae]

XIII

It is the time of the last time.
My body has already returned home:
I am walking down 42nd Street keeping time
to the neon city of lights
—"Naughty, bawdy, sporty ..."—
and I recall one of those love-blind
Tin Pan Alley ballads
with which my American self wooed you
in your twenty-third year
—"All or Nothing at All"—

As we pass from the Via dell'Anima
into the piazza
to write the figure of valediction
in the eros of drifting
for the last time
as you, Flavia, hold me by the hand
I cling with my fingers
to the point of no return
vaguely at play in your exquisite limbs
as it hardens into the verdict
of a silent and tremulous kiss

Fixed to the embonpoint
I must now sever myself
from the spectacle
that still fascinates me

In this fatal city of the many Romes,
I won and lost you,
bride of Roman fever.
Day by day, night by night
you translated my exile

into intimacy and ardor
in this great labyrinth
without a center

I shall now cover the world
as a fugitivus errans
and shall remember
only the amorous architecture
of your caress

The minor games of pronouns,
of tourists and young lovers
—the Three Coins and the Bocca della Verità—
have lost their magic force

Flavia

To cross the piazza
we play the final set
of a more wicked game
odi et amo
truth or dare
the discrepancy
between sympathy-love and passion-love
the écart of love at last sight
the last kiss, soave fanciulla,
the sting of which
transposes addio into exile,
the aria into verdict
even our great accomplices,
wild discourse and *parole pellegrine*,
turn into the reproachful
stuttering of the techno-pedant
—aphanisis, meta-Italian,
the *italiano mancato* of the seersucker—
and banish me
to be procreated
in the West of desire

—Arrivederci, Roma—
here begins the real exile:
the eternal apprenticeship of gaps
and the unending wait for your signs

Tired out by the night of
anomalous passions
and illicit pleasures
Santaccia, accompanied by her equipage
—the Shades of Love
who have never succeeded
in taking her virginity—
crosses the deserted piazza by
executing a lazy-eight

Does she Santaccia,
orphaned daughter of Venus,
mother of Aeneas and Rome,
address you or me
when she, vestal and she-wolf,
breaks the silence
with hysterical laughter?

Your silence tells me:

    enter the temple of Venus genetrix
    with dangerous thoughts
    for all true love must die
    mark this day
    with both a white stone,
    and a black stone

Santaccia's laughter,
her wicked and raucous stornello,
a detour through which
the vestal becomes the she-wolf,
tells me something else:

    play DEATH
    —la petite et la grande—
    play AMOR
    —the sacred and the profane—
    play the RAPTUS
    —the thunderously loud moment of ecstasy
    that the piazza alone confers
    by refusing to be crossed …

[Matins]

the piazza as mandala

FUGUES

Slow Apocalypse

the earth is within me
and now my dance has measure

Ceremonies of Change: A Fugue for Wanda Landowska

Sic Transit Gloria Mundi

Landowska
took
for her medium's mouth
a mantic chain of teeth
occulting the sun's drum-fire cadences
with the rubato of the vague moon …
for her canonic art
the zigzag of intrepid hands
playing the remainder of midnight
against itself,
repeating antagonisms of voice
into ceremonies of change …
for her discipline
anarchic branches
of God's descending tree
weaving like perpetual hair
the fierce thread of a fugue

Weaving being a part of women's writing …
Penelope and Clytemnestra
weaving backlash and homecoming
all womb-weaving the weightlessness of the child
or white-writing the bride's laughter that explodes
from the grain of salt on the tongue
to spike the bachelor's inky serenade
—bubble, bubble—
all weaving/writing,
like Landowska at the keyboard,

the free beauty
of the fugue that,
in searching for its ending,
cuts through the limits of desire
or inscribing,
with musical fingers,
nocturnes and parades
into the empty, monotonous line
to release
the torrent of rhythm
and that which resists it
—broken-chords, deadlocks, hoverings
(this trembling web of stop-time gerunds
and participles)—

Oh you free lovers,
whose passion moves faster than music,
do you not become one
with the suspended beauty
of the vibrato?
Oh you lovers of variations,
are you not cut and edged
by the forbidden figures of enjoyment
that breach the great silence
with the force of desire?

The anima, the bride of the wind,
contriving freedom into a symmetry …
weaving even when unraveling
the splendid shroud
that furls the wilder adventure
of her who to voyage
remains in place …

Weaving even when triggering,
like a Cassandra melancholy at the jukebox,
the blanks concealed in the clavier,
straining the metronome of the severe father,

the mustachioed inspector of well-tempered time,
and with a rogue thumb
wild on the black keys
staining the milky way
with the dark tremolo
  of shadows

And where Isadora
spun with gestures
and oriented space
around her parable-body
and Garbo transcended
the pretense of face,
Landowska drove fire
through a scarecrow's hair
into intricacies of light,
threading the needle's eye
with silence

with silence

    seeding mantras into

                    boundaries of sound

from silence

    releasing the furious rhapsody

                    of a thousand and one particles

                                of stolen time …

(This poem was set to music by the composer Michelle Ekizian and premiered on 14 February 1998 as "Ceremonies of Change: Concerto for Piano and String Orchestra" by the San Francisco Women's Philharmonic Orchestra and the pianist Gloria Cheng.)

Baedeker for Etruscan Places

For Dante Matelli

the meriggio goes barefoot like zero
even the lizards recoil from the white-hot world
taking the scampering noonday demons with them
the daylight cannot assume its masks of shadow—
the excesses, the hurl of things …
anti-rhythms
and then measures of Etruscan deaths

their stanzas dance suppliants
in the necropolis
of the unconscious
threatening to displace
your amorous writing
with more arcane images:

        fish grows into horse

        red sodomizes pink

        the bull of asym-

        metry
                gores the slender world
        into copulation

my changeless body
drags its dialectic
of a lingering animal
from the white noise of the open
and shadow-dives into a grave of space

some vermilion gesture
all poses and proffers
the self-begetting egg
that world hides the changes
of fire and water
the vibration of space and silence
invents the reckless body
it ravishes the brides of quietness

the lion changes the gazelle
with ancient ornaments
stars of blood
symmetries taken by chance
ricochet of the glass world
mirror more furious and complex
with color
ascending, bursting
with the weight of cinnamon
and its skeleton
blonde as a concubine
that tiptoes and renews
clasped Bacchants swerve
nonchalant with violence
—image and corpse—
of inverted lyre and tresses hooded
with wind

vehement with transparency
these bodies break through
the surface of the frescoes
now their dance
plies the seam of consciousness
the seem of art: the mimesis of death
truth
the metonymy
that links
scene after scene
to death

and its terrible dislocation
through metaphor
beauty
the eternal artifice of hymen
that con-
founds inside and outside
extravagancies of beloved and lover
dream and phallus
the chiasm of sense
that alone disseminates death
the history of metaphor: the genealogy of death

white the orgasm of black
two-personed time
bawd of symmetry
sidereal yet addicted to death
allows the clinamen:

    of generation and contrast
    the blue-backed dolphins
    deviate
    through the invisible net of waves

(Tarquinia, 1973)

The Cabaret Singer: The Metamorphoses of Bianca

For B.B. who goes slumming the night
before her debut at the Met

MI CONTRA FA DIABOLUS EST

do you sing, casta diva, for me
or just for the company of midnight tenors?

is your soft rehearsal, a torch song
for romance or for afterwards?
now you release your bel canto fatigue
in an earthy bistro laugh
that modulates into a chanson

it darkens my sense
your persona
and its violence
of eyelashes and nostrils
what strangenesses of blue
slash and stint
in your deep song

keyhole scenes array themselves
forced by a judas desire
no longer mine
pantomimes of the savage father

—top-hatted and cyclopean
chez Le Boeuf sur le Toit

retro-daddy, saltimbanque
of the French leave,
Jack of the curtain-lecture
wedlocked to the harangue,
Arlecchino of the laughing body,
neither fish nor flesh,
not yet Hemingway nor F. Scott,
cuckolder of the daguerreotype,
magnifico of the *paradis farouche*
and the vaseline symphony
caught punctually by Brassai,
roller of the bones of Paris-dice—
is it always to be his yang
his nocturnal salt, chrism, christcross, silk
his gunshot, ricochet, breath, silence …
souffleur! prompter! Dionysokolax!
bastard patrimony
of hidebound enchantment this:
all skin is already his hieratica: X

is it Mistinguett you play
displaying the abyss
of a wheel
that digs with acid and mascara
into the onyx of each eye
his my thy?

voice
that tears itself
wild and vague
every spacing
deepens a deathrattle
then once again
everlasting ravenous and quick
sucking at the sun
dodi dodi

FA MI SOL FA MI SOL

the sirens
anterior women
and slight muses
would give endlessly
the big dance of the sun
or the gnosis of black wings
the stain
the velvet of numbers
or the violence of hymen
and not this rictus of rhythm
this blackout of sense
this dowry of black
whiteness that forces the music
of the world's worlding
into a deadlock

the tribal women
MARIAS
madonnas of diphthongs
their songs were green
and cadenced like olive trees
I hear forever their profiles
suffered the cut sky
child-held and passaged
through their fecund syllables
through ululation civilized
by the eternal return of the sun
their sterile pregnancies made voluptuous
with Ave Maria
repressed prayer exploding
        into hyperbole:
the cow is milked
through the wedding ring
the fearful apparent
shivering in its rite of hands
one seizes the rhythm
of nihil
by the throat
forcing it into gender

the soul another kind of skin
the blank that narrates the body
and when I unfastened her,
I found that her strong sense
remembered the certain faces
and meticulous jasmine
of those plain songs
and that to break all unison,
I am her supple body,
I am her bandit rib
and the verging shape
of her hands

lightning from the skin
my nostalgia, the madrigal body,
you refine me instead with dissonance
rifts and nuances
dancers of white numbers
you engender in me
and finally silence
with your blue note
the persistence of the mothers
for whom the sibilant earth
and its sotto voce
continue the cradling shape
—pietà—
of their lustral bodies
and their furiously exact
litany of cicadas,
the voice-cry
of requiems
without deaths

your contralto deranges me,
Adam of never agains
into the blanks of desire
suddenness I cannot follow
the tritone unleashes a counter-song
wild with stain and shadow and nicht

that breaks up the certain world
by more than love (or resistance)
you bind me to the radiance
of carnal shards,
the runes of your haywire laughter
—mana, manna, obscure milk—
you trace yourself now all over again
in this mask of black writing
infinite parody of the white line
you breathe
vera icon
the white eyes of death
dominoes
la morte ficcata:
your extreme pledge:
bis

at last you cast off your masquerade
to become Bianca (whom I can know)
you exit from the kicker lights
and shatter the scrims of cigarette smoke
with your nice curtsy
of a country girl
the vacancy is foreclosed
by the shock of applause
then as you remove your long black gloves,
the canny patter
with Caliban at the pianoforte
maestro of rigamarole and
the tts-tts-tts-tss-tss-tss-tss of dives
and like Prospero
you abjure rough magic
and leave vengeance to your fierce sister
parallel muse
recumbent and lascivious
bourgeoise and slow
secreted in the cabaret of night

MI FA SOL? MI FA SOL?

Across a Crowded Room: A Portrait of the Cabaret Singer as Unscripted Artist

For the "Devastating" Lynne Charnay, Muse and Femme Fatale

All that has dark sound has *duende*, that mysterious
power that everyone feels but no philosopher can explain.
—Federico García Lorca

"Let's Do It, Let's Fall in Love"—
with a de-lovely voice
staggering to the staccato
of Cole Porter's delirious rhymes,
the marquee singer at the Café Carlyle
coaxes her upper-set audience
—"birds, bees, and even educated fleas"—
to be teleological
—jacket required;
   optional but recommended:
   eternal love bracelet by Cartier—
but the real command is
to fall in love with her darling voice
Do the bon bons of its cadences
allow the listener a choice—
love me, or love me not?

I prefer to fall for the soul-storms
unleashed by the cabaret singer's
devastating voice

chez Don't Tell Mama
—that cozy and tight boîte
where
the unscripted diva Lynne Charnay
deviates from all those obligatory
where-or-when, body-and-soul protocols
to summon the *duende*
as if for the first time—

when
like an angel trying
to free her wings
from the mud of temps perdu
her dark voice searches for light
as it cascades her listeners
into the cabaret of the heart—

where and when
the wild cadenzas of her sultry voice
obliterate the distance
between sound and sense
only to conclude with whispers that impart
bitter-sweet lessons in the art of love,
anti-Valentines that
—unlike those tear-stained ballads
standardized with stardust—
reveal the catastrophic lines of desire
  that mark the eternal struggle of love's body
  to reconcile Amor and Eros—

when and where
she plays the femme fatale
who charges her phrasing with
"lascivious grace" and discordant harmonies
to unsettle torch songs into existential chansons
that accept the lacerations
of l'age mur
without regret
and in defiance of the traces of time—

where and when
the rhythm and timbre of her search
for the blue note release
the millions of poems in her voice,
her tenebroso
always resonating with intimacy
as she finds her voice by losing it,
always expressing her will to interiority
even when instressed
by the enchanting dialogue
with her virtuoso pianist
or made to throb in response
to the occasional duet
with her sublime basso lirico,
even when she shifts her persona
from chanteuse to diseuse
to frame her arias
with naughty but cosmic chit-chat—

when and where
by praising tears and affirming
the rough magic of love of love
as she courses through her diverse repertory,
she extends "Les Feuilles Mortes,"
her signature chanson,
into a more comprehensive September song
that overcomes memory's fallen leaves and fallen loves
and celebrates the eternal return
of those amorous fade-outs and silenced voices
that the Blue Angel had dismissed with the refrain:
"I can't help it."—

when and where
she expresses her will-to-birthdays
by celebrating the inevitability
of one more candle
in a voice resounding with desire
as it twists its way

between being-for-love and being-for-time
to declaim amor fati with bravura
as did her sister La Môme Piaf
although she detonates the Sparrow's blast
—"Non, rien de rien"—
by other means and in other registers
—the vocal aberrations of pithy ditties
and her panoply of surprises,
including the shock of laughter
and the less conspicuous provocation
of laughing up her sleeve
as she deconstructs those tear-stained ballads
that in the good old days
used to float nonchalantly
in that soigné cocktail comprised
by Peacock Alley and its pianoforte—
(Can a diva be Nietzschean just off Broadway
and when removed by a century
and a grand ocean
from Le lapin agile and Le chat noir?)—

where and when
the chanteuse becomes a muse
by breaking her voice to break
the humdrum magic spell of midnight
and by ransacking the déjà entendu
to lead her audience
of sibyls and retro-dandies
to transform
claustrophobia into ecstasy,
echoes into prophecies,
hearing into listening—

Do those soul-storms
in which passion and
exacerbated melancholy carouse
allow the listener a choice—
Devastate me or devastate me not?

Do or Don't tell Mama
that the dangerous *duende*,
that necessary demon,
has ravished you this night
and aroused your élan vital?

Reality as a Triptych by Caravaggio

For Idanna Pucci and Terrence Ward

Yet I am the necessary angel of earth,
Since, in my sight, you see the earth again.
—Wallace Stevens

Painting is silent poetry, and poetry is
painting with the gift of speech.
—Simonides

… For beauty is nothing
but the beginning of terror, which we still are just able to endure,
and we are so awed because it serenely disdains
to annihilate us …
—Rilke, *Duino Elegies*

Every work of art is an uncommitted crime.
—Theodor Adorno

In its implications, the distortion of a text resembles
a murder: the difficulty is not in perpetrating the deed,
but in getting rid of its traces.
—Sigmund Freud

Prologue: Upon Receiving Grace from Viewing *The Seven Acts of Mercy*
at the high altar of Pio Monte della Misericordia

How is the contemporary viewer—
necessarily secular even if a believer

and for whom "God is dead"
at least for the second time
and whose aesthetic sensibility
has been deauraticized
by the despiritualization of art
and the deletion of its numinosity—
to express gratitude for the grazia ricevuta
from paintings created over four centuries ago
by an artiste maudit and
a technician of trouble and wildness
such as Caravaggio
for whom the sacred illumination is embedded
within the profane illumination;
for whom the epiphany is generated
not only by the representation
of the sacred violence of the God-event
but also by the violence of painting
through which reality is rendered an event?

Caravaggio as a painter and a man
was an angel of violence and
in *The Seven Acts of Mercy*
that violence is expressed formally
by the folding of the vertical into the horizontal,
by the folding of light into darkness
to create the infinity of chiaroscuro,
by the folding of the chaos of sixteen figures
into the order of the seven acts of mercy,
by the folding of the sacred into the profane
by which the ordinariness and materiality
of the profane is sacralized.
Caravaggio's religious paintings
—above all, *The Seven Acts of Mercy*—
require their viewers to be necessary angels
in the sense elaborated by Wallace Stevens:
"Yet I am the necessary angel of earth,/
Since, in my sight, you see the earth again."
In *The Seven Acts of Mercy*,

we see the earth in the faces, gazes, and bodies
of the Neapolitan street people
that Caravaggio used as models
and transformed into compassionate
auratic figures;
we also see the earth
in his own solicitation of Mercy
for his transgressions
through the grace conferred by painting

The Calling of Caravaggio: A Litany for Saint M (Michelangelo Merisi da Caravaggio)

They said people can't pray in front of a killer's paintings.
–from Derek Jarman's film *Caravaggio*

According to the other scripture,
the negative one begun by your rivals in art
—your contemporaries such as Giovanni Baglione
who was Salieri to your Mozart
and then forwarded by those reactionaries
who followed in your wake
and remained fixated upon
the certainty of the classical style
such as the Arcadian Poussin who, in 1657,
blasted you for coming into the world
to destroy painting
and formalized in 1672
by Bellori in *his Lives of the Painters*,
who asserted that your dark style
violated the majesty of art—
you were a maestro of recklessness
and transgression,
a wicked man, according to Stendhal,
a Black Michelangelo,
more a murderer than a saint.

The real murders you perpetrated
were in the distortions of your paintings
that wreaked havoc
on the "regulative 'mapping' aesthetics"

of Renaissance Classicism
and, more importantly,
by which the profane was rendered sacred,
the boundaries between the earthly world
and the heavenly realm obliterated,
and the invisible and defaced bodies
of the lower class made visible
in a way that disrupts and overturns
the class gaze of those papal and patrician patrons
who feted you nonetheless.

You were and forever remain
the prophet of the plebes
who annihilates the gaze of your spectators
and your true art of *terribilità*
lies in getting rid of the traces
of these gaze murders,
erasing them in the *tenebroso*
and the sacred violence of light.

your great lessons:
light may be only accessed through darkness;
grace only comes through violence

The Calling of the Spectator

Instructions to My Gaze:

As I stand once again
before Caravaggio's "triptych"
dedicated to St. Matthew
in the Contarelli Chapel,
in the Church of San Luigi dei Francesi,
I wait for the tribe of tourists to depart
after they exclaim "Awesome!",
their New Age amen,
and then take Selfies,
their way of genuflecting
before the trinity of masterworks.
They were captivated by the banalities
of the lecture delivered by their tour guide
who attempted to historicize them
in ten minutes
by explaining the effects
of Caravaggio's Baroque theater
and the imperative of the Counter-Reformation
to grab the attention of the Catholic viewer.
He concluded with a *tartufo*
for the neophytes,
a tweet on Caravaggio's
contemporary canonization as the third man
—L., M., C. (Leonardo, Michelangelo, Caravaggio)—
and his lionization
as rock star and Saint Bad Boy
that results from the postmodernist retrieval
of his work and legacy.
The *cicerone* might have added:
In the beginning was the *Stoss (Stoß)*
—the shock of the Caravaggio effect—

i.e., Caravaggio's art of sacred terrorism
—to Hell with Renaissance form;
seeing must become being—
that defined and galvanized the Baroque
but also paved the way for
the modernist aesthetics of shock.

A missed moment:
no trigger warnings
about the ransacking of the viewer's gaze
unto astonishment
and the derangement of the soul
by the shocks of illumination
confronting those who witness
Levi/Matthew's conversion
from sinner to saint
in three acts;
no mention of the tremendum
nor of the numinosity
by which the ordinary spectator
—even if an atheist or agnostic—
is rendered a retro-catechumen
by bearing witness to the Christ-event;
no mention of the badassery
at work in Caravaggio's style
by which the spectator is converted
by the event of painting
into a catechumen of art;
no mention of the voguish question
raised by contemporary art historians
—"Where is Matthew?"—
which renders the painting
into an aporetic experience
by positing that the figure
traditionally identified as Matthew
is a dislocation
and that Matthew is actually the young man,
shrouded by shadows,

sitting at the end of the table
who is obsessed with money
and refuses to respond to the divine emanation.
The tribe needed to wrestle with this question
for it might lead to a corrective
and subliminal counter-reading
that sees the young man
as the shadow in Jung's sense,
the dark side that the traditional Matthew
must acknowledge as he accepts
the call to change his life.

—for Christ's sake,
should not the evangelist of hyper-tourism
have challenged the tribe
to do soul-work
by opening themselves
to the epiphanies
experienced by Matthew,
including his calling to death,
and to perform gaze-work by locating
the shocks, the aporias, and the puncta
in the enigmatic and disorienting paintings
by which the viewer
is inserted within the Divine Drama
in which the spheres
of the aesthetic and the religious collude?—

So much for the safe aesthetic experience
within our Babelian Age of Kitsch
and its routinization of shock.

After having viewed the paintings
periodically for over half a century,
will I experience the fear and trembling
of the first viewing
when I had come to Rome
to receive the catechesis of *la dolce vita*

and found, instead, the *horror vacui* of the Baroque?
Will I be able to become an anti-tourist
and philosophical pilgrim
by resurrecting Kierkegaardian inwardness
and by confronting the triptych
as a limit-experience?
Will I be able to follow Matthew's leap of faith
—albeit proleptic or suspended in the *Calling*
and then enacted in the *Inspiration* and *Martyrdom*—
by witnessing the event-Christ existentially
and thus religiously?
Caravaggio positions the spectator
within three scenes of seeing.
In the *Calling,* Matthew's gaze
responds to the advent of Christ's gaze,
and he finds his way to kenosis and metanoia.
We see by seeing Levi/Matthew
seeing Jesus
seeing him
and enlightening him
with grace—
the light that comes
from the transcendental elsewhere
to penetrate the raunchy and profane space
of the tax office that resembles more closely
the backroom of a tavern
or a set in a film noir avant la lettre?
But we also see by assuming the gazes
of those who do not see
—Matthew's entourage
of dandies and hangers-on
who respond either
indifferently and frivolously
or refuse to behold,
namely, the two figures to Matthew's right
who are obsessively focused on money
—with usura the line of sight grows thick—

Will I be theologically attuned enough
to respond to the silent calling
of the "inverted dialectic"
embedded within the triptych?
In beholding the paintings,
will I be iconoclastic enough
to kill my inner Pharisee
—iconoclastic as was Caravaggio,
who putatively came to destroy painting
but who, in fact, theologized and sanctified it
by glorifying earthbound reality
and, like his cinematic successor Pasolini,
comprehended the revolutionary and militant
nature of Christ
as first documented by the
Gospel According to St. Matthew
and ultimately by the
Gospel According to St. Matthew
According to Pasolini?
Will my gaze be sacralized
by Caravaggio's realism
that refuses to accept
the separation of the sacred from the profane?
Will I accept Caravaggio's call to see Otherwise
and to respond to the call of painting?
Will I experience the three crisis states of Matthew
by facing the initial question
posed by the penetrating light
and seconded by Jesus' words
silenced by the painting
—"Follow me"—
and then reiterated by the finger pointing
of Christ and St. Peter
to which Matthew responds gesturally
by fingering his fallen self
—"Who, me?"—
a question in response
to the surprise of the call

that becomes much more decisive
—Who am I? Who was I? Who shall I be?—

Will I place myself into an eternal crisis
even though I begin the travaille of gazing
by stuffing coins like a Publican
into the machine
to activate the artificial lighting in the dim chapel,
the very coins inscribed with pagan figures
that Levi/Matthew, the tax collector,
counts out
somewhat avariciously
with the fingers of his right-hand
as he receives the call?

Viewing Caravaggio is
to be broken by light
and to be blinded
and rendered bouleversé
by the darkness that gives light.
Darkness is the accomplice
and apostle of the light.
Without the apophasis of chiaroscuro,
grace comes not.
Caravaggio's scripture:
Let there be Chiaroscuro,
the darkness that enables the light.

LAZZI

**Lazzi* (from the Italian *lazzo*, a joke or witticism) are stock comedic routines that are traditionally associated with Commedia dell'arte.

—Wikipedia

The Lazzo of the Hiccup

Ach! mitten im Gesänge sprang Ein rothes
Mäuschen ihr aus dem Munde.

[Ugh! Right in the middle of her singing
A red mouse sprang out of her mouth.]

–Goethe, *Faust*

Never recite
—even when passionately solicited—
a poem, wicked or sublime,
trobar leu or trobar clus,
to guests after supper
for ineluctably
the most beautiful of all
—Tanya this night—
will take to hiccuping
and dazzle the Tribe of Ben
with the sudden art
of the soufflé and its collapse:
her image ever more breathtaking
as it shatters and recomposes,
chastely wanton
and to be imbibed slowly
like the brandy of the devil

The Lazzo of Z

For the Madonna of Boleros

HAPPY BIRTHDAY ...

Zaniness is simply an instance
of your perfect pitch and is no less cun-
ning a part of your music than lines and
rhythms and harmonic colorations.

If I play the desperate song
of my exile like a twelve-bar blues,
it is because you have caught me
at the point when one cannot
be loved any longer.

If I mistake the lighted fan
of your window at the Casa Rustica
for the swoon-haunted moon and
search for *pizzicati* in your music,
it is because you as keenest music
alter the limits of the world.

And if I take your laughter
in re maggiore for a torch song
it is because desire fails to measure
the distance to be covered when
Winter covets Spring.

We may not return to Stravinsky.
But know that bawdy summer consummates
in its arpeggios the meeting of extremes
and jasmine-haunted August releases
its nuptial song in the breathless form of a bolero

... TO YOU

Lazzo of the Manhattan Matinee
or, Seduction Manqué

Still on Roman time after all these years,
I am unfashionably late
for our rendezvous in Manhattan.
No matter—
you are caught up
in some cellular phone intrigue
about a book launching,
your body gossiping like a high-strung diva
in a grand finale,
as you slowly move toward the very edge
of the proscenium,
bower of shadow,
covered by the green canopy
of your new uptown digs
on West 110th Street just off Broadway
and far from your beloved downtown bohemia

Still inclined after all these years
to the saltiness of Roman straight-talk
à la Martial and Belli,
your chevalier wonders whether
he will lose a language to you.
After executing a reckless u-turn,
I pick you up at a gallop
in my Marinetti-mobile
—a black spyder with the top down—
as you perform a charming *croisé devan*
to greet me at the curb.

All seems to go well—
the salute, the handshake of souls,

and even my little test
in the form of a blague
—"Will-you-permit-me-to-keep-the-top-down-
even-though-winter-is-in-this-first-day-of-spring?"—
"Yesissimo!" you say.
I press down on the accelerator
and James Dean it downtown
Another buzz and you ask for pardon.
The intrigue requires you to be a decipherer
of elaborate Tribe of Ben protocols.
Are you testing me as I tested you?

Still in the Marinetti-mobile,
we breeze through Central Park
via the 97th Street Transverse
—*intentionalität* of the wind,
activating the pastorals in your name, Phyllis,
shepherdess of almond trees and breeze.
My response to losing my breath:
a double-clutch.
You descend from the chariot,
as in an apotheosis by Tiepolo
and your spikes resound
like madrigals on the concrete
of the sidewalks on Carnegie Hill.
You applaud my rebellion
when I put a quarter in the expired meter
where a stranger's Maserati is parked
just as the meter maiden is about to issue a ticket—
"Desist, Medusa, that car is much too beautiful
to profane with one of your bureaucratic billet-doux
from his majesty Bloomberg."

Sitting opposite each other
in banquettes at Sarabeth's,
you speak in measures—iambic pentameters—
that wrap me up in the intricacies
of your cosmic chit-chatting.

I am all eyes,
but out of old-school gallantry,
I try to avoid the mystery
of your pale Pre-Raphaelite face
and the beguilement of your eyelashes,
noticing discreetly that you are dressed
as poetically as you speak.
The crab cakes, precariously placed on top hats,
require a different sort of decipherment on your part.
Out of sync I order breakfast for lunch
—ricotta pancakes—
and pommes frites for the table.

Then the walk down Fifth Avenue
to the Jewish Museum
to view the scandalous exhibition.
I surprise myself by naming
all the Nazis in the rogues' gallery—
Does that make you wary of me,
your "monumental gentile" beau?
Sensing your sense, I assume the persona
of an ornamental gentleman caller
and then recite chapter and verse from Adorno.
Our reactions to the exhibit tweedledee and tweedledum—
Tweedledee: Angst all over again; Angst uber alles!
Tweedledum: Kitsch all over again; Kitsch uber alles!

As we walk downtown on Fifth Avenue
hand in hand
—reluctance in your gait—
I sing "*Che gelida manina*"!
Then the Neue Galerie—
After we check out by rote
the sweet black chairs by Adolph Loos,
the Klimt paintings
on the second floor
return you to life—but not to me—
Then we are mesmerized by Oskar Kokoschka

and his "Portrait of Dr. Tietz and his Wife."
What strange vibrations and filigrees
pass electric/elective affinities between husband and wife!
What a perfect gloss to our matinee!
When will we finally kiss?
Will we ever Kokoschka?
Will our bodies ever Klimt our souls,
and will our caress be passionate enough
to replicate the one portrayed
in "The Kiss" and be dangerous enough
to break the boundaries of the golden mosaic
in which the artist has enframed the lovers?

Yo and Nes
Edam and Ave

Will this matinee become a nocturne?
Will this day that ends
with the courteous gallantry
of a well-placed farewell kiss on your hand
inaugurate a season of enjambments?

The Lazzo of the Neapolitan Howl

Io sono napoletano, e se non canto muoio.
—Libero Bovio

I have seen Naples and died a thousand times;
I have heard Naples a thousand times and died only once.

Like Pulcinella always in search of the Subrisio Salatorum (the smile of the acrobats), I found myself on a spree to Delirious Naples with a collegial group of art historians when I was a Fellow at the American Academy in Rome. The art historians were hell bent on visiting the altar Filomarino in the church of Santi Apostoli in Naples and other specialized works that would confirm their connoisseurship. There we were in the Baroque church ecstatically inspecting Borromini's gaze-boggling altar, and all of a sudden a funeral procession barged in and took possession of the nave. Unlike in America where the coffins are placed on wheeled devices, here everything was left to the unsteady casket bearers—hunched-over like martyrs—who dropped the coffin onto the stone floor. The fierce sound it made was like a nail driven into the universe—the thump of death that silenced silence. Then the women mourners emitted a series of cosmic howls expressive of their grief that threatened the pedentives of the dome. It was all too much for the thin-skinned, prim and proper scholars, putative masters of time and the terror of Caravaggio's dark spaces, and they immediately fled through the side entrance to find the emotional security of the outside. I was the only one who stayed, compelled by a Proustian involuntary memory precipitated by those earthquaking howls that brought back to my mind the explosive and exaggeratedly melodramatic expressions of true grief I had heard as a young boy at the funerals of family members in Manhattan.

I genuflected and made the sign of the cross, thereby recovering my Neapolitan body and soul, even though the howl I emitted was silent.

The Lazzo of the "Schiava Turca": Parmigianino at the Frick

Painting is poetry that is seen rather than felt,
and poetry is painting that is felt rather than seen.
—Leonardo da Vinci

Imparmigianare: to submerge expression of the
subject in elegance and delicacy.
—John Shearman

Carissima donna ispiratrice,
you whose name I cannot name,
in channeling your enigmas,
must my gaze
darti del tu or *del lei*?

And have those enigmas
been engendered by you
as a protean subject,
an intriguing and elusive sitter
who astonishes yourself
with the *sprezzatura*
of your self-presentation
or by Parmigianino
who has rendered you
as a fascinating and ravishing object that,
although imprisoned within
the inanimate discourse of painting,
presents the splendor and dangerous magic
of your truth as a sentient being who flows?

Your finding of yourself as a woman
enables Parmigianino to find you
and your viewer to find you by losing you.
Which of you is the supreme Mannerist
—the true maestro of finesse?
Do you *imparmigianare* Parmigianino
or does he *imparmigianare* you?

Are you a *signorina* or a *signora*?
—pardon this query whose subtext violates
the decorum of the Perfect Courtier—
and, more to the point,
are you a femme fatale
who will ransack my desire
or a cryptic angel
whose burst of innocent laughter
as promised by your coy smile
will hurl yourself into my soul?

Your title—*The Turkish Slave*—is a misnomer,
an interpretive error made centuries ago
by a scholastic cataloguer at the Uffizzi
who Orientalized you by mistaking
your exquisite Renaissance chapeau
—a well-crafted *balzo* (headdress)
in the aristocratic mode of Isabella d'Este—
for a women's turban,
whose folds must always be flagrantly ad-libbed,
and also by fancying in your
exotic white ostrich-feather fan
the whorls of a dervish.
Had he but seen the fan-fare at play
in Isabella's *lazzi*
in the *Commedia dell'arte,*
such a parapraxis
—a Freudian slip of the gaze—
would have been precluded.

But the myopic pedant's
greatest and most blasphemous gaffe
was to misconstrue the gold chain
on your right sleeve as a mark of slavery,
thereby expressing his repressed desire for you
by thrusting you into an imaginary harem
and sentencing you to sexual slavery.
This solecism cannot be pardoned
neither as an expression
of Renaissance geopolitics
—Turkey as the sign of otherness and the exotic—
nor as an involuntary expression
of his scopophilia
—his phallocentric fantasy of a pasha—
for it violates your grace
and deletes your muse-function
and your autonomy as a woman.
His misprision is a nomenclatural murder
that attempts to erase your soul and nobility.
Your contemporary viewer
while humming Mozart
must "abduct you from the seraglio."

Your vendetta for the pesquisador's canard:
your sweetness does make you a Turkish Delight;
your wild folds are those of a whirling dervish,
even though you remain motionless and silent.
Besides ...
your viewer will be your slave
as was "the little one from Parma"
riveted to the roulette of your smile
and mesmerized by the arabesques
of your aristocratic costume
and the coup de force of your gaze
that breaks the fourth wall.

I shall whirl with you
and find ecstasy

in the concentric golden folds of your *balzo*
and in the curlicues of your brown hair
that protrude from it.
I shall spin with the flourishes of your raiment
and grow dizzy from the convolutions
of your indigo blue sleeves
and the white madness promised
by the fluffiness of your fan.
—this intoxication of your viewer's gaze
begins and ends with the meanderings
in the mise-en-scène of your countenance
and in the whiff of desire
one detects in your ethereal smile—
you have ravished and conquered Parmigianino
and inspired him to devise
exquisite mannerist conceits and surprises
that ravage your beholder.

I shall find alchemy
—yours and Parmigianino's—
in the intricate gold threads
that run through your elegant regalia
and that propel your viewer's gaze
to cascade down your half-figure,
beginning with the gold emblem
at the center of your *balzo*
that punctuates its carousel of golden folds
and then followed by the horizontal golden stripes
of the white silk partlet that covers your shoulders
only to disclose the temptation
of your slightly exposed breasts
and culminating in the almost imperceptible
gold ring on the fourth finger of your left hand
that points the way by default
to the gold chain embedded
within the blue sleeve covering your right arm.
The glittering stream of gold
evinces your incandescence

and proclaims your nobility.
The true courtier
such as the humanist Pietro Bembo,
attuned to hieroglyphic meaning,
would be outraged by the sequaciousness
of the small clique of contemporary art historians
who, to counter their fear of enthrallment,
commit the obscenity of dogmatic stupidity
by automatically associating
the color gold with prostitutes,
thereby de-fascinating you
and erasing your upper-classness
by imprisoning you within a stereotype
—as did the cataloguer long ago—
when your aura demands
the struggle of unending gaze-work
and the special questioning of Hermes
that leads to the interminable analysis
of a dangerous hermeneutics.

I shall find poetry in you
and danger in your canny smile
and in your suggestive décolletage
as intensified by the estro
of the wildness prefigured by your plush plume
and break off my imaginary affair
with the mystery of Mona Lisa
and the serious magic of her uncanny flickering smile.

How then am I to ascertain your proper name
in the intricacies of your masquerade?
Or is it Parmigianino's masquerade?
Are you a muse or a *cortigiana onesta*,
a siren or a trickster?
Are you an aristocrat whose garbo
or a coquette whose flirtation
are both activated by Parmigianino's
mannerist deviations
and the play of his visual metonymies?

Such futile questions only confirm the
serio ludere of your game
—as redoubled by Parmigianino—
that animates your viewer's desire
with the undecideable.

Where am I to find the lineaments
of your desire?
They are, of course, proclaimed
by your art of fashionable dress
—After all, you are a *quaintrelle avant la letter*—
But you write your identity
through the secret language
of your silence and namelessness
and through your beauty as conveyed
by the perpetual mutability
of the nuances of your facial expression
and the gentle twists of your body
—Do you stand or sit?—
You graciously and seductively return
your viewer's gaze
and thus become la belle dame avec merci
even though you disrupt your beholder's "image-repertoire."
But you also assume a posture of self-command
that affirms your cachet as a woman who knows thyself.
Parmigianino has made you sparkle
and thus empowered you to command the last gaze
and to have the last word.
Are you the amorous subject or object?
You are a cynosure rampant with surprises and flashes
—a cynosure is a cynosure is a cynosure—
The light strikes from the left side of the painting.
Why are you so oblique,
your head twisting slightly to your right,
your body to your left,
offering us only one of your ears to behold
and shadows gently descending down
your face and neck?
Do the inflection of your eyes

and the curve of your smile
maintain an eternal dialectic
or just constitute a fugitive moment?
Does your facial expression as accentuated
by your slender eyebrows
and the radiance of your rosy cheeks
promise a love story or a blank message?
Bis: are you the amorous subject or object?
The tip of your nose and
the tips of your elongated fingers
disclose by concealing
the antinomy of Amor and Eros.
Your short neck is that of a soprano
and thus far removed from the mannerist madness
of the *Madonna dal collo lungo*
and the deviations of Antea, your sister.
Your supreme cynosure:
the exorbitance of your fan,
an emblem linking the restraint of aristocraticness
to the wildness of the id,
leads your viewer to imaginary desire
that sets into motion the free play latent within your plume
—your viewer must go mad—
if only Queen Elizabeth I (played by Flora Robson)
in an old black-and-white Hollywood swashbuckler,
had witnessed this coup de théâtre
that takes place by not taking place,
she would have abandoned
her frivolous bandying about
of an identical white plume.

Your viewer is forever condemned
to the augury of the game of thy name
—Aimee Ng, the sagacious and astute
art historian at the Frick,
has passionately limned the golden emblem
at the center of your *balzo*
in which winged Pegasus,

—as white as your fan—
boldly strikes the earth,
causing Hippocrene, the fountain of the Muses,
to gush forth and to release the flow of creativity.
And thus Pegasus became the sacred horse of the muses,
the symbol of poetry and your emblem.
This led La Ng to postulate that you were a poet,
possibly Veronica Gambara
—a beau geste that triggers an understanding
of you as something more than a "glass of fashion" and
permits your viewer to know one of your secrets—
that you have searched to find
the right word to finish a line
and to create metaphors to trigger love
just as you have sought to devise
the strophes and slant rhymes
that define the poetry of your fashionable dress

—Women who write must dare to have wings
and thus are the most dangerous of lovers
for they must refuse to remain
"unravished brides of quietness"
by ransacking silence
like the Maenads tore apart Orpheus
—is your white fan an oneiric metaphor for the pen
with which you write in black ink?—
Nonetheless, I shall always remain entrapped
within the hocus-pocus
of the no-exit game of the sobriquet—
The Madonna of Ekphrasis will do for now
for your viewer is compelled
to write a passionate poem for you
whether by the silence of gazing
or by mounting Pegasus by lifting a pen
in the name of the sacred muses
—a motet or madrigal to capture your fugue
rather than the trap of a Petrarchan sonnet—

And ultimately
when the game of thy name blacks out
and becomes the game of thy namelessness
and after Boiardo's card game
with the deck of Tarocchi
exhausts the twenty-two possibilities,
this viewer will call you Diotima
for you propel your beholder
up the scala d'amore,
the Platonic ladder,
ironically called klimax,
that leads from incarnated
and sensuous beauty
to the idea of beauty,
even though it is written
in The Courtesan's Diary:
"Down with Plato! Viva Aretino!
—for he who sees you must die—

Let us raise our imaginary *balzi*
and our plumed top hats
to you, Lady Soul,
who "imparadises" our mind's eye
and to your gallant accomplice Parmigianino
whose futile alchemical search
to solidify mercury
was already realized in his portrayal
of the quicksilver of your lineaments
and the incandescent folds of your soul:
Here's to the mannerist high
and to the finesse by which
it keeps sub rosa
the pledge of yourself
and your love
to silence!

The Lazzo of the Mondrian Detour

For Stephen R. and Susan S.

My accomplice in the coup de dés
that sets words into freedom
and comrade in singing
the counter-hegemonic blues,
the incomparable Lucio,
supreme artist in both
abstraction   and   realism
who constantly defies the kettle logic
that divides them
and virtuoso of the Duchampian swim
—a wicked DADAyama of death by water
   within a sea of white paper
   in honor of Rrose Sélavy—
kindly invited me to join him
for a pranzo to be held
at a breathtaking studio
—vertiginous and archaically avant-garde—
on 38 Bank Street in NoHo
on the condition that I keep a secret
about a certain metamorphosis
known only to myself and three others

(Aside to Arlecchino:
The *lazzo* must conceal a secret
from the quidnuncs)

The rite of introduction—
the usual pastillage
even through spoken in resonating Italian

I compliment
our congenial hosts
—daring artists,
   even in their collage as husband and wife—
on the height of their sublime ceiling

Incipit the *lazzo*:
Thus Sprach Arlecchino
—a dissertation in double-talk
accompanied by pantomime
on my theory of how high ceilings cure
the insomnia to which writers are prone

The husband confessed that he suffers
from the insomnia to which painters are prone

Then the delectable velvet
of spinach soup punctuated by a crostino
from a classical recipe by Marcella Hazan
—the *lazzo* of the maîtresse d'hôtel
proclaiming her bravura as a chef

(My inner *lazzo*
that I necessarily keep secret:
Freud's wicked dream of spinach)

First Pizzicato:

I indecorously blurt out another secret:

My family only buries their dead
in Ferragamo shoes.

(it elicits the rumor of suppressed laughter)

Second Pizzicato:

The husband graciously shares his work:

Two white paintings
—constellations—
punctuated by tiny black marks …
demonstrating the existence
of fifty shades of white,
a Mallarmean exercise
in activating palimpsests—
black holes in the form of whiteness

Third Pizzicato:

The wife even more graciously shares her work:

Three assemblages using found objects
that generated geometric shapes
—trapped in culs-de-sac—
in bold colors
gold,
red,
blue,
and even her husband's white …

I perform the *lazzo* with my gaze

Final Pizzicato:

After complimenting her
I suggest that the most stunning
assemblage
should be titled:
The Mondrian Detour

(The marriage of their incongruous works
has liberated me
from the conjugal vendetta
Freud had secreted
in the detour
of his contentious dream of spinach envy

for even dead ends and
the soft lozenges of spinach
can release the convulsive geometric jazz
and the danse sauvage of colors
of the *Broadway Boogie Woogie*)

THE DEATH OF THE DANDY

Blue Sonnet
or, Sonnet that Hides your Name

—Keep to the darling protocols of the fling—
rightly by the proper of your fair eyes
am I instructed, and the fairer thing,
darker increase, fired out to sonnetize.
Con grazia: the bloodline of gaga sighs
must I well temper to fit the refrain
of the virginal and quicksilver's thighs
to the clavier's finesse by w(r)it restrain.

Con alcuna licenza: such bravura
I cannot urge from my rough instrument
all tensed to the hurdy-gurdy's violence.
Why, when you, fictor, strive to free women's sense
from your idiot husband, the novel omnipotent,
compel me to fidge this darling form—Charbovari?

For Ungaretti:
Portrait of the Virile Poet as Senex

We need used words to modify our youth
tracing in us Adam's intact desire.
We need the old man's remembering
to bring us to our beginning
by devouring his archaic dreams—

dead desert mirages animating …
meridian fables, satyr-words
pastorals of desire …
trees of dense shade nymphs incarnat-
        ing …
dream ikons into present distance ab-
        stracting …
carnality of dreams opening …

We need the old man to beget in us an
        aurora
shattering the secularity of repetition—

        originating dawn,
        apocalyptic dawn instressing Adam's
        day,
        binding us to the commencement,
        waking mind to the day's ideal body.

We need the old man to recover
our antique rhythms—

        physiology of lost rhythms …

subtraction from anterior silence,
syllable added into song,
endecassillabo, sestina enduring our an-
archy,
liberating us into the obedience of time.

Word within a word
Dance within a dance
Penelope within a star

The poet measures secret into secret,
mediates through a glass of words
inequalities of light—
incipient star and Baroque sun.
The ascesis of hyperbole: to carry the sun
in a cup.
The poet keeps the dawn pure,
sees suffered into cyclical stone of universe
the beginning sensuality of woman's face
and diffuse curve ↓
nuptiality of morning.
The poet cannot forget remembering—
here Phaedrus and everything already echo
and even silence an interruption.
The poet remembering continues us,
remembering Christ into unicorn of pity,
stars into fables bereft of Odysseus,
woman into a tree of dream,
figures absolute of silence into
gracious fingers of word and rose.
Landscape is not rhetorical,
the world is not invented,
no paraphrases of the sun.
The sun is an epiphany loosened
into its own language—suddenly.
Innocence is not a myth or a preceding myth

or what an Adam-dark dream constructs,
but the Dream itself …
circumference, precinct of light,
mask of light,
emblem forever doubling our first images.

Once upon a time
Blazing a beginning analogy
Ungaretti perpetual in the sun—
Repose of sun.

Epitaph for a Trickster

For Thomas Belmonte, shape-changer,
who like Vertumnus, dancer of walls,
loved the things Pomona loved
and who, after lifting the last disguise,
revealed the radiance that became what Pomona loved;
For Tommaso, ethnographer of Naples
and serene guide through the drunkenness of its labyrinth,
who, upon exiting the broken world,
smiled back at the crippled boy, Ribera's double,
and conferred a valediction to labyrinths:
"Be grateful for what is offered. Go lighthearted into Paradise";
For Tom, lover of wisdom and trickster,
always already remembered in Diotima's emblem of Love,
always already remembered in Cavafy's words:
"Remember, body, how they trembled for you in those voices."

Blonde-Night, Lost-Labyrinth Radical Blues

lost my sense of timin', rhymin' & ontologizin'
one bohemian espresso-house midnight
on Bleecker Street sometime after '68
and just before the Cafe Au Go Go closed down

... found sweet Ariadne in that radical night
but the hard, no-exit labyrinth
was nowhere to be found
for the nocturne of the new Lost Generation
in its search for a surrealist night
had released the freedom of the infinite dialectic
and the demand for the impossible

—Ciao Hegel! Ciao sublation and all dead ends!
Go Rimbaud & poetry in the streets!
Go Gramsci & revolution in the streets!
Go Allen Ginsberg & Flower Power in the streets!
Go Valerie Solanis & sexual politics in the streets!
Go Carla Lonzi & feminist revolt in the streets!
Go Richie Havens & freedom in the streets!—
To hell with boundaries!
Demolish all labyrinths
(real or imaginary, visible or invisible, cultural or psychic)
and undo the Borromean knot!
Il est interdit d'interdire ("It is forbidden to forbid")
as the Parisian 1968ers used to howl—

after their raucous march
and the sounding of their "barbaric yawp,"
the anti-war protesters—me too—
had returned to occupy the Village
in order to crack the night

assuming their other (i.e., counter-cultural) bodies
as hippies and jouisseurs,
they refused the command of the Big Other
—a.k.a. Mr. Backlash—
and as they drifted
—Situationists without knowing it—
down West Houston to defy the curfew of geometry
by walking on water to cross the Hudson River,
the rhythm of their hot moves
performed a *derive* that proclaimed
—the Unconscious is structured like jazz
   and rock 'n' roll music … not Language—
   even the Minotaur turned beat
   as he hit the road
   to join the "pissing multitude"

although seated within the flickering confines
of an antiquated café
where the avatars of Hemingway and Fitzgerald
enacted their moveable feast Greenwich-Village style,
she seemed to be dancing madly
with the hip moon
as she, too, searched for a surrealist night

—outside the post-beatniks and pranksters
on their way to becoming the Blank Generation
staggered by as they rummaged around
for "reality sandwiches"
and headed up to the Café Wha? to make the scene
but the actual happening
was in the wild high of the streets
where they attempted to encounter
the man who ate fire for a living

… connected to her by one overheard word
directed to her entourage of literati buddies
—crypto-bourgeois—
followed by an espresso command

perfectly pronounced to the waiter
—"*Un caffè corretto alla grappa, per favore*"—

lost my sense of underin', overin' & inbetweenin'
her sweet gaze penetrated me like a stiletto
and her blondeness enveloped me like the Scirocco
her wild silence tasted as Dionysian as absinthe,
provoking me to violate
the bourgeois line between tables
so as to initiate a cosmic chit-chat

we spoke incessantly about existentialism
—his and hers—
and Marxism, classical and Groucho tendency
(e.g., the "creative destruction" of *Duck Soup*)
and the dictatorship of Coca-Cola,
the opium of the people,
and the tactics and anti-strategies of the Situationists

I maladroitly blurted out my version of a reality crack
—the story of a random encounter with Sartre
chez Les Deux Magots in the early summer of 1962
in which he ferociously interrogated me
for over an hour to determine
whether my New York college-boy politics
passed muster with his

—aye, tutti-frutti and groovy Greenwich Village!
aye, undeconstructible even though
always exploding Greenwich Village!
where everyone is a permanent revolutionary
where every one triumphs over *horror vacui*—

... even though strangers
in that convulsive night
we became partners in singing
the counter-hegemonic blues

lost my sense of nowherein', meanderin' and lazy-eightin'
... after the poète maudit
'Go Rimbaud' routine lost its pizzazz,
took her uptown to tango at El Morocco
whispering in her ear Lacanian sweet nothings
and first-kissed her with the force of diamat

she was the soft labyrinth
and the sweet thread was her blondeness
pulsating and deviating in the midnight air

lost my sense of timin', rhymin' & rhapsodizin'
... took her to an uncanny lecture at Columbia
by the forensic William Burroughs
who raged on about how Kool-Aid acid
was poisoning the reservoirs Upstate
and long after the love me or leave me caresses
had become a protocol,
she invited me
—on the condition I dressed in a rich boy's suit—
to a concert to meet Minos,
her imperious and clubby Big Daddy
whose cyborg handshake rocked my hippiedom
and then, after mispronouncing my name,
his gaze rattled the surface of my Dagotude
by misconstruing
my Marinella tie for camp
he queried: "Have you managed to bring
the war of position to the Philharmonic tonight?
Did you kill the Moonlight Sonata tonight?"
I fired back: "How is your quest
for 'reality sandwiches' going?"
then as a conventional Babbo
anticipating the future,
he asked in falsetto: "Does your family throw
confetti or coriandoli at weddings?"
I popped back: "They hurl metonymies."
he chuckled and then we bonded
agreeing to kill our inner Minotaurs

… lost sweet Ariadne
somewhere in the multitude of Times Square
after one of our usual bouts of flânerie
in search of a surrealist night blacked out

… entered the hard no-exit labyrinth
—she took the subway into midnight,
her sweet violet perfume jitter-bugging
on the asphalt with what remained of the moonlight
and then memory turned into a soft labyrinth
threaded with traces of blondeness,
a *labirinto cieco* whose darkness was inter-
rupted by flashes of the dialectic

ELEGIES/EULOGIES

For a Gentleman and Scholar Dying Young

In memoriam Douglas Gardner Caverly

Those fields at Lawrenceville were Elysian.
I cleated them only in the dark jersey
of a visitor;
you glossed them daily with jukes
as if they were the odes of your beloved Pindar
who taught you that athletes write victory poems
with the *arete*
of their hazardous moves and slant rhymes
and, whether on or off the field,
must avoid *hubris* at all costs.
And when, in our syllabus,
Homer's "wine-dark sea"
turned into Joyce's "snot-green sea,"
we scholar athletes,
under the post-Olympian tutelage of
our bohemian mentors
on leave from Greenwich Village,
learned that preppies qua jocks
were obliged to express their hostility
toward their opponents
in a gentlemanly way by shouting:
"Bloom is a cod!"
Those aristocratic academies prepared us
to remain golden boys
—freewheeling and free-spirited
even though our bodies remained
constrained by J. Press blazers and regimental striped ties
and our disciplined tongues
tied to the scansions of dactylic hexameter.

When we moved on to college chez the Upper Left,
we were expected to embrace the mission
of becoming New York intellectuals
and anti-preppy radicals.
I accepted the call while you resisted it,
remaining resolutely preppy *in perpetuum*.
Throughout our splendid friendship, however,
the gentlemanly protocols of jockitude remained intact.

Our first conversation—mostly in Cod Latin—
took place when we were both post-postgraduate students
in the grips of the rite de passage into professorships.
The event, crowded with scholars of all stripes
and hoity-toity Manhattan mandarins,
was more like a "nose-picking" (sic) seminar than a fête.
We withdrew into a huddle and began
an intoxicating and rambunctious conversation
through which we managed to "kill the spirit of gravity,"
as Nietzsche would say.
We started with a flippant quip
about how writing sonnets was
like playing tennis,
after football your great passion.
You then gave me an acute tutorial on
Lucretius' notion of *clinamen*
immediately lapsing into jock talk in which you
applied it to the swerves at play
in the Hail Mary passes you lived and died by
—and Pindar bestowed his approval.
I then described my brief days as a
college basketball player
for whom playing hoops in the1960s was
a primary means of integration
Although a bit under six-feet,
I could surprisingly (even to myself) dunk,
and the crypto-racist coach would tell me:
"Hey Pilgrim, we're going
to make a white man out of you."
I responded cryptically in English-major fashion:

"Coach, *Go Tell It on the Mountain*,"
an allusion to James Baldwin who used to hang out
at the West End Bar in those post-Beat days
—my way of telling the coach in palimpsestic Latin:
"Vaffanculo!"—
You laughed and said Pindar would bestow
his subtlety blessing upon the retort,
and we drank a toast to the "inimitable one"
which you proposed in the original Greek:
"I deplore the lot of tyrants."
Incipit our infinite conversation.

Did you know back then
that Parnassus would be Wall Street
and that Eden turned into Peacock Alley
at midnight when the paramours parsed
the dactyls of a Cole Porter song?
Disconsolate Gatsbys,
we became comrades and brothers.
I told you that Fritz Lang had correctly placed
those fields at the vertex of Metropolis
—the black-and-white capitol of capitalism—
where the rich boys cavorted
as jocks aroused by femmes fatales.
You told me, breaking off your recitation by memory
of one of Pindar's victory odes
and miming the great Trimalchio in West Egg:
"No fortune in America was created
without the fear of catastrophe."
I would remain forever confined
to the cordon sanitaire of academia
where I unthreaded the texts so beloved to you;
you left the "small world"
and its pretentious intellectual games and
went to the World Trade Center
where, despite the greed and the need for abstract labor
and the hunt for the Arcanum of the commodity,
you remained a humanist

always faithful to Pindar's refusal of *hubris*.
You married a beautiful woman with a loving intellect
and fathered a handsome son with a loving intellect
who would find his way out of Preppiedom
as he constructed and measured out his universe,
and who would write surrealist poems
on the soccer field with the shocks
of his daring moves, slants, and zig zags
(and to whom I passed on
my time-worn basketball jersey
for old-school good luck).
You exchanged your blazer for
a Brooks Brothers pinstripe suit
punctuated by an ancient madder tie
and transformed your Latin and Greek syntaxes
into the obligatory Manhattan lingo
and prosaics of making a deal,
although the eruption of Pindaric eloquence
perpetually threatened your proems and codas
just as the Vesuvian death of Pliny the Elder
used to explode into the memory
of Pliny the Younger.

On February 26, 1993, the terrorists bombed
the World Trade Center for the first time,
and you were wounded unto a slow death.
Pindar would lament,
saying that scholars and athletes must not die young.

In your epilogue:
the splendor and *sprezzatura* of a gentleman
and the *gravitas* of a classicist in all things—
May you finally resolve the enigmas
of Pindar's hermetic verse
by dancing to the dithyrambs
of his victory odes.

Elegy for "The King of the Bay"

In memoriam Luciano Rebay

Your departure, friend of my soul,
has made me lose a language

I hear you swimming silently,
disappearing in the ocean of my mind

Will you speak to me once again through silence?

Or is that the point of death
and the guilt it imparts to the survivor—
to oblige us to respond to someone
who no longer responds?

Silence also speaks
and it alone is stronger than death

I do not know where and how
to bury my memories of you

My memory shall await for your signs
to appear in the intermittences
between alba and aurora
that you taught me to read
so attentively
so assiduously

I shall refuse to settle
for the randomness
of involuntary memory—
the fluted and plump petites madeleines

the cobblestones of Venice
and all that Proustian jazz

I shall solicit your signs
deliberately and ferociously
with the daedal desire
of poetry
drawing the dangerous flame
of memory
from the feints and hesitations
of rosy-fingered dawn

I shall ransack silence
and in its fragments
I shall hear your aria once again

A prayer not for your repose
but for your journey
—May you continue down routes of ecstasy—

We will forever remember you
as the great-hearted, great-souled
KING OF THE BAY
who like Ungaretti's *lupo di mare*
mastered the joy of shipwrecks
and who like Montale recognized
within himself the hazardous law
of the Mediterranean Sea:
"to be vast and various and yet fixed."

Requiem for a Roman Nose

Ave Maria,
Gratia plena,
Dominus tecum.

Tonight Aunt Marie
—our Mimi, our Riri—
died in the hospice
—Grande Hôtel de l'Abyme—
of the Mother Cabrini Hospital
at the age of ninety-five.
A soprano now without her beloved tenor,
her last aria was voiced through silence
and we witnesses performed her death scene
as if characters in the finale of *La bohème*
although our arias of heartache remained mute.

She was the last to depart
of the four fabulous Bello girls
who grew up in Sinatra-ville—
bobby-soxers who became femmes fatales,
they were noted for their irresistible
and convulsive beauty
and voluptuous Neapolitan bodies.
Like proper Neapolitans
they loved love
and died when they did not sing.

Their spirits were as ecstatic as volcanoes
—cheerful in the Nietzschean sense
although they did not need to read philosophy
to enact *amor fati*—
Their perpetual laughter contradicted their sad brown eyes,

inherited from their ancestors
—the Great Mothers—
who had carved their masks for millennia
to face the fatality of the Italian South.

They never wore black but dressed
like movie stars of the forties
in colors like toast and ginger
—the color of the interior of Radio City Music Hall—
Anna Magnani was their emotional archetype
although their dangerous beauty
was more like that of Sophia Loren
and like divas they ransacked the "Image-repertoire"
of their suitors.

> *Benedicta tu in mulieribus,*
> *Et benedictus fructus ventris Tui,*
> *Jesus.*

Like all quotidian saints
Mimi left little to be commemorated
in an obituary.
How is one to account in words for a loving intelligence?
When a child I said to her:
"Aunt Marie, tell me something about your mother."
She responded:
"She was a saint—a goddamned saint—she had nine children ..."
And then, "Tell me something about your father."
"He was a very healthy man."

She dismissed as *cafoni* those swains
who serenaded her with "Oh Marie."
She broke the heart of the mad Doctor Mensalullu
notorious for his violations of *garbo*,
even when dancing the jitterbug,
and whose shirt cuffs protruded too far
from the sleeves of his ill-fitting sharkskin suit
to qualify as a gentleman and lover.

She married a passionate and compassionate man
who found her adorable,
addressing her always as "*soave fanciulla*."

She dreamed of being a soprano
and assumed the role of her namesake in *La bohème*
at my mother's *serate musicali.*
Toward the end, she listened incessantly to Puccini arias
and thought they were the music
that would be played in Heaven.

In her last years, she kept her mind alert by
playing enigmatic word games.
At the last moment at the hospice,
she first spelled out our names
letter-by-letter and
then pronounced each of them decisively.
We misconstrued this as her way out of dementia
and back to us
when it was her valediction and blessing.

The *commare secca* had ravished her countenance
out of jealousy.
Only her magisterial Roman nose remained intact
—now a rudder to guide her rigadoon
with the angels who nose-dive
in Giotto's frescoes in the Arena Chapel,
tracing their auras into the lapis lazuli
as they go from glory to glory …

Sancta Maria,
Mater Dei,
Ora pro nobis peccatoribus
Nunc, et in hora mortis nostrae.
Amen.

Acknowledgments

Rome became my home as soon as I saw it. I was born that moment. That was my real birthday.
—Federico Fellini

Thirteen Ways of Crossing the Piazza is a collection of poems written primarily over the last three decades, although a number of them were created earlier, including my first published poem dedicated to the great Italian poet Giuseppe Ungaretti (*Books Abroad*, 1970), who was my mentor when I was a Fulbright Fellow in Rome and whose poetry was the subject of my dissertation. We became dear friends, and I served as his cicerone on a number of his forays into Manhattan. I want to express my profound indebtedness to him for our walks through Rome during which he lectured me on the Baroque and for serving as a role model for writing poetry in which concealment becomes disclosure. Since the genesis of the book has been so long, I have too many debts to acknowledge here. I ask pardon from those I fail to mention, a number of whom are treated in poems dedicated to them whether explicitly or implicitly.

I wish to express my wild gratitude to my three necessary muses and eternal friends — Lucio Pozzi, Frank Lentricchia, and Dante Matelli — for their exquisite contributions to the genesis of *Thirteen Ways of Crossing the Piazza*. All three of them have inspired and encouraged my writing in vital ways. I am particularly indebted to Lucio Pozzi, incomparable artist and Duchampian trickster, who has blessed the book with seventeen dazzling drawings in black-and-white and one in color that have forwarded the dialogue between poet and painter we began in *The Fat Man Arpeggios* (Guernica 2015). His astounding and uncanny illustrations will enhance the reader's encounter with the poems by foregrounding the interplay between poetry and visual art and by activating the transferences of *ut pictura poesis*. Frank Lentricchia, supreme literary critic and brilliant novelist, has been my first and most attuned reader—an Ideal Reader in Umberto Eco's sense who has gifted me with incisive criticism, thought-felt advice, and sweet encouragement. I shall be forever beholden to him for the brio with which he has sanctioned my attempt to write "anti-professorial" and eccentric poems in the name of Wallace Stevens and

Wittgenstein and the unutterable. His recent validation has both humbled and galvanized me and might serve as a gloss for reading the poems: "Your poetry proves that the representation of the real can only be accomplished in wild language." Dante Matelli, my Italian "brother" who lives in Rome, has guided my attempt to learn from the Eternal City. After his long career as a provocative journalist for *L'Espresso* during its heyday and his bouts as a prize-winning screenwriter for Marco Ferreri's *L'ultima donna* and *L'udienza*, he has turned to writing fiction — short stories and radically experimental anti-novels such as *Ermes*. He has been my companion in crossing the piazza ever since we were graduate students and my constant mentor in comprehending Italian cultural and intellectual life. He appears as a character in several of the poems. And finally I wish to acknowledge my indebtedness to Michael Mirolla, my passionate and visionary editor at Guernica and fourth muse, who has once again honored my poetry by housing it within a beautifully executed book.

The book was generated by a long and rapturous involvement with Rome where, for a good part of my life, I have lived, studied, meditated, drifted, feasted, caroused, experienced the melancholy of its ruins and the horror vacui of Baroque art, and befriended countless Romans of all stripes—philosophers and "foolosophers", revolutionaries and tricksters. These encounters have been integral to my attempt to learn from the Eternal City—no easy task for, as the proverb puts it: "Roma non basta una vita" ("Rome, one lifetime is not enough"). Therefore, I wish to express my profound gratitude to Rome for giving me this book of poetry and for bestowing upon me those sacred and profane illuminations that have enabled me to become a poet by expressing my great love for Rome as emblematized in the palindrome ROMA/AMOR (ROME/LOVE) with which the text begins.

And to be more topographically specific, I wish to acknowledge my indebtedness to the Piazza Navona where I used to reside (Via Santa Maria dell'Anima 16) for teaching me the art of crossing the piazza, thereby engaging me in what Jung called "the circumambulation of the self." At the heart of the book are thirteen Roman poems set in the Piazza Navona that describe the happenings in the piazza as a way of exploring the "rough magic' of the cityscape of the Eternal City and of confronting the paradoxes and aporias through which the piazza happens as a private and public space—most enigmatically, how the piazza takes place by not taking place. The exploration of the piazza as an interactive space/place is part of a more comprehensive attempt to stage a profound political, cultural, and, above all, existential encounter with contemporary Italy.

And finally, I should also like to acknowledge my indebtedness to the Fulbright Program and the American Academy in Rome for granting me year-long fellowships in Rome. Both have been definitive to my intellectual and cultural formation. As previously mentioned, the Fulbright blessed me with the mentorship of Ungaretti and also with unforgettable anecdotes that have generated a memoir—"The Anecdotes of the Red Ferrari"—that will be part of the book on writing and desiring Italy that I am now completing. My time as a fellow at the American Academy was glorious as a result of the camaraderie of Joseph Brodsky, Donald Barthelme, Roy Lichtenstein, Edward Hirsch, and many other distinguished artists and intellectuals from various fields in residence. (Pardon the name-dropping.) What resulted was a compelling year-long interdisciplinary dialogue on the culture of postmodernity and the so-called triumph of theory in the arts and philosophy then underway. That infinite conversation involved a crucial encounter with architects that has determined my teaching and creative life. I had previously been honored to have translated Manfredo Tafuri's *The Sphere and the Labyrinth* (The MIT Press), one of the canonical works of twentieth-century architectural history and theory. Joseph Connors, then director at the Academy, staged a luncheon in honor of Tafuri and a number of other architects. The conversation with Tafuri and the other architects was unforgettable. It also generated invitations to assume visiting appointments at a number of graduate schools in architecture where I lectured on architecture and cinema. It led me to the supreme folly of simultaneously writing two books dedicated to crossing the piazza—the present book of poems and a companion volume that treats cinematic Rome and the crossings of the piazza depicted in iconic city films from *Rome, Open City* through *La Grande Bellezza* (in press). I should like to thank my architectural colleagues, especially Robert Mangurian, Mary-Ann Ray, and Joan Ockman, for heightening my architectural consciousness in ways that have informed the writing of the poems and their attempt to write space and place, and to confront the psychogeography of Rome through drifting and risk-taking—the problem of crossing the piazza and, at times, its refusal to be crossed.

And to those who will read this book, I hope the poems will both sing and dance for you. If you suffer, as I do, from a terminal case of "Roman fever"—the Roman equivalent of the Stendhal syndrome—the poems may be of use to you in working through your obsession and fascination with Rome, for they attempt to confront the dangerous pleasure —the jouissance—that Rome confers upon those who attempt to encounter and to desire it. If you are a wayfarer or pilgrim trying to overcome the melancholy of crossing the piazza after midnight (the very melancholy conveyed by the shot of the character played by Gina Lollobrigida in the film *La Romana* with which this book begins) or an archi-tourist suffering from "piazza-envy," they may lead you to comprehend the spatial/temporal and existential risks imposed by Piazza Navona—the quintessential piazza and metonym for Italy—that requires those who traverse it to move beyond flânerie and to become anti-tourists and philosophical travelers. I should add that, as a counterpoint to the Roman and other Italian-based poems, a number of the poems are set in Manhattan and are dedicated to exploring what being a New Yorker entails. I hope they will lead you to channel your "inner New York" without killing it. Perhaps the poem dedicated to the celebrated cabaret singer Lynne Charnay will encourage you to attend one of her performances chez Don't Tell Mama that will definitely activate your "Manhattan fever."

About the Author

Pellegrino D'Acierno is deeply committed to boundary-crossing interdisciplinary and theoretical work, and he defines his intellectual project and teaching mission as belonging to the humanities—both in the traditional sense of the term and in his own rather personal definition of it: to take the risk in one's intellectual and creative work of never arriving. He has maintained a dialogue with various disciplines, having challenged and troubled his disciplinary identity as a comparatist and Italianist by teaching and writing on philosophy, cinema, art history and architecture. Although as a writer his initial medium was prose, including work on a number of screenplays, he has turned to poetry as his "late style"—a dangerous conversion because poetry involves an exile from ordinary language and always demands a confrontation with the unutterable that activates the poem of silence within the poem of words. He has also attempted to dialogize his cultural and intellectual identity by encountering Italy, something that has doubled his "median state" (Edward Said) by rendering him an exile when in Italy and an exile upon his return to America. *Thirteen Ways of Crossing the Piazza* contains poems set either in Rome or Manhattan and thus presents a tale of two cities through which he explores his conflicted identity and the displacements that define his life and work.

D'Acierno is Distinguished Professor Emeritus of Comparative Literature and Italian Studies at Hofstra University, where he has been honored to serve as the inaugural Queensboro Unico Distinguished Professor of Italian and Italian American Studies. The chair marked the culmination of his career-long attempt to render Italian texts central to the curriculum of the American university. Columbia University has recently named him a member of its Society of Senior Scholars, and he continues to teach in the Hofstra Study Abroad Program in Venice.

Educated at Columbia University (B.A. 1965, M.A. 1967, Ph.D. 1973), he has a long history of teaching there, having held an assistant professorship in Italian and Comparative Literature (1973-1982) and, more recently, visiting professorships in three different graduate programs: Italian; Architecture, Planning and Preservation; and Comparative Literature and Society. He has also held visiting professorships in various fields at Cornell and New York University, and in the graduate schools of architecture at Yale, Rice and the Southern California Institute of Architecture. In 2006, NYU named him as the first holder of the Tiro a Segno Visiting Professorship in Italian American Studies.

He has been awarded fellowships from the Guggenheim Memorial Foundation; Villa I Tatti, the Harvard Center for Italian Renaissance Studies; the Italian Academy for Advanced Studies in America at Columbia University; the Fulbright Program; and a Prix de Rome in Post-Classical Humanistic Studies from the American Academy in Rome. In 2009 the Rockefeller Center at Bellagio awarded him a fellowship that enabled him to undertake the writing of *The Labor of the Negative: Italian Philosophical and Theoretical Culture from Vico through "Weak Thought"* (forthcoming), which contains all of his previous work on Vico and Gramsci, the two thinkers who have inspired his project as a critical humanist and poet.

His publications in prose include: *F.T. Marinetti and the Freedom of Poetry* (1988); *The Itinerary of the Sign: Scenes of Seeing in Giotto's Frescoes in the Scrovegni Chapel* (1995); *The Italian American Heritage: A Companion to Literature and Arts* (1998): and *The Signature of D'Annunzio and Other Counter-Essays on "Dagotude'* (forthcoming), a collection of (im)personal essays. His interdisciplinary work on the relations between cinema and architecture will appear in two installments: *Thirteen Ways of Crossing the Piazza: Rome as a Cinematic City* (2019), a study of the topos of the piazza in Italian city films and thus a sequel and companion to his Roman poems, and *Strange Loops: Cinema and Architecture as Spatial-Temporal Practices* (forthcoming). He has translated Manfredo Tafuri's *The Sphere and the Labyrinth: Avant-Gardes and Architecture from Piranesi to the 1970s* (1987) and edited or co-edited three other books: *C.G. Jung and the Humanities: Toward a Hermeneutics of Culture* (1989), *Delirious Naples: For a Cultural History of the City of the Sun* (2018) and *For a Dangerous Pedagogy: A Manifesto for Italian and Italian American Studies* (forthcoming).

Guernica Editions published in 2015 his first book of poems—*The Fat Man Arpeggios*—which paved the way for their publication of *Thirteen Ways of Crossing the Piazza: Collected Poems* (2019). Both books have been illustrated by the incomparable artist Lucio Pozzi, and the dialogue between poet and visual artist—something of a rarity these days—has defined both works. He is currently completing a new book of poems—*Anti-Haiku Moments and Profane Illuminations: The Exorbitance of Italy*—which treats the excessiveness of Italy and the impossibility of fitting the epiphanies it bestows within the seventeen syllables of a haiku.

About the Artist

Lucio Pozzi is a New York artist who now shares his time between Hudson (NY) and Valeggio s/M (VR) studios.

He was born in 1935 in Milan, Italy. After living a few years in Rome, where he studied architecture, he came to the United States in 1962, as a guest of the Harvard International Summer Seminar. He then settled in New York and took the US citizenship.

In 1978 the Museum of Modern Art, New York, exhibited his early videotapes in one of the first single-artist exhibitions of the Projects: Video series. He occasionally writes and has taught at the Cooper Union, Yale Graduate Sculpture Program, Princeton University, Maryland Institute of Art, School of Visual Arts. He currently is a visiting instructor at art schools in the US and Europe. His work has been presented at Documenta 6 (1977) and at the Venice Biennale (American Pavilion) in 1980. His art is represented in many private and public collections.

Pozzi was honored with a National Endowment for the Arts Fellowship in 1983. He received a Master Honoris Causa from the Accademia di Verona, Italy, in 2010. Premio Ciampi L'altrarte 2015. Premio Lissone 2018, Career Prize.

While painting is the core of his art, Pozzi is a secretly subversive artist. The first scandal came in 1978 in the temple of Conceptualism, the John Weber Gallery in New York, when he exhibited landscape watercolors a few months after having presented there a giant installation of a constructed wall and a photograph, both having a part cut off and relocated on them. When he then assembled the first Provocation Show, in 1980, again at Weber's, the critical response was so embarrassed that hardly anyone dared comment. Many thought Weber and Pozzi had gone mad. The show consisted of 80 works all related to painting but radically different from one another in form and materials. That show was followed by large exhibitions of the same kind in public museums and private galleries: at University of Massachusetts Amherst, in Bielefeld and Karlsruhe, at Studio Carlo Grossetti, Milano, and in 1984 a three-gallery show in New York (Susan Caldwell, Leo Castelli, John Weber). Still now, Provocation Shows of Pozzi are occasionally set up by some museums and galleries, while exhibitions of only single families of work also continue.

It seems that since those years many diversified artists' practices have been accepted in the artworld, but Pozzi's persistence in painting both apparently abstract and representational works, constructing photographic entities and concurrently producing performances and building installations and making videotapes appears to be receiving interest mostly among the very youngest generations.

His teaching is another way for him to question and probe the fabric of modern art making, in a subtle, individual, case by case dialogue, a capillary manner of guerrilla infiltration instead of shouting sensational slogans or producing grandstands.

MIX
Paper from responsible sources
FSC® C100212

Printed in November 2019
by Gauvin Press,
Gatineau, Québec